W9-AOV-373

30 Days
to a More Incredible
Relationship with God

from *Today's Christian Woman* magazine

Edited by
RAMONA CRAMER TUCKER

Tyndale House Publishers, Inc.
WHEATON, ILLINOIS

Library of Congress Cataloging-in-Publication Data

30 days to a more incredible relationship with God / edited by Ramona Cramer Tucker.
    p.   cm.
    "TCW books from Today's Christian woman magazine."
    ISBN 0-8423-0590-4
    1. Christian women—Prayer-books and devotions—English. 2. Spiritual life—Christianity. I. Tucker, Ramona Cramer.
BV4844.A123 1998
242′.643—dc21   98-23842

Printed in the United States of America

03 02 01 00 99
10 9 8 7 6 5 4 3 2 1

CONTENTS

INTRODUCTION

Do you wish that

- you knew for sure God was listening to your prayers?
- you could approach the Lord without feeling guilt due to your past?
- you had a job or ministry of more "eternal value"?
- you didn't feel so spiritually "blah"?
- you could give your worries to God and experience real peace and rest?
- you could share the good news of Christianity more comfortably with your friends, relatives, and coworkers?
- you knew *why* God was allowing you to go through a difficult time?

If you have spiritual questions like these, you're not alone. We all wonder why God doesn't "grow us up" into the faith more quickly instead of letting us gain so many bumps and bruises, and why our prayers sometimes seem to bounce off heaven's walls.

This book provides practical encouragement for growing close to God. It will help you pray with purpose, discern what's Christian from what's not, find security in your heavenly Father, and turn anxiety and doubt into deeper faith and trust. And that's just for starters!

Each day provides a Scripture passage; a story or message; a quote from a person such as Elisabeth Elliot Gren, Joni Eareckson Tada, Jan Dravecky, or Carol Kent; and reflections on a topic, as well as "A Step Further" to help you grow in that particular area of spiritual life. In addition, the "Faith Focus" will help you evaluate how you're currently doing and where you'd like to be, and give you ideas on how to get there. The "Prayer Pointer" will assist you in focusing your prayers on the topic for the day.

In just thirty short days this book will give you footholds that can transform your walk with God—and enrich other areas of your life and relationships. Scripture promises that if we seek God, we'll find him (Jer. 29:13). So let's be like the apostle Paul, who said, "I am focusing all my energies on this one thing: Forgetting the past and looking forward to what lies ahead, I strain to reach the end of the race and receive the prize for which God, through Christ Jesus, is calling us up to heaven" (Phil. 3:13-14).

Ramona Cramer Tucker
Editor
Today's Christian Woman magazine

WE CAN BE CONFIDENT THAT HE
WILL LISTEN TO US WHENEVER WE
ASK HIM FOR ANYTHING IN LINE
WITH HIS WILL. AND IF WE KNOW
HE IS LISTENING WHEN WE MAKE
OUR REQUESTS, WE CAN BE SURE
THAT HE WILL GIVE US WHAT WE
ASK FOR.

1 JOHN 5:14-15

*D*o you ever wonder if God is *really* hearing your prayers, or if they're bouncing off heaven's walls?

I certainly do—especially when nothing seems to be going right. It's on those days, when I'm feeling really human and I begin to doubt God's listening skills, that I open my Bible to verses like 1 John 5:14 (see opposite) and James 5:16 ("The earnest prayer of a righteous person has great power and wonderful results"). If you, too, sometimes wonder if God is listening, this devotional will give you the confidence to approach God with purposeful prayers.

Praying with Purpose

There was nothing remarkable about the phone call. But it marked the beginning of a small crisis of faith.

When I picked up the receiver, my friend said, "Did you hear Susan had her baby? I hate to tell you this, since you had such a hard time in labor, but she got to the hospital at 9:30. About 11:30 she told God she couldn't stand any more. Little Dorothy was born thirty minutes later."

What did God have against me? I wondered. All my life I've been surrounded by people who seem to receive dramatic answers to prayer. When my friend and I both prayed and fasted about what college to attend, she got a clear response; I decided for myself, or so it seemed. When my grad school friend needed seventeen hundred dollars for tuition, she received it through an anonymous gift; when I needed money, I got a job.

Does God have a double standard, treating some believers better than others? Or does he simply not hear our prayers? After hearing about Susan's easy labor, I was in danger of becoming a prayer agnostic.

But when I sat down and analyzed my doubts, I wondered if perhaps my whole concept of prayer was wrong. It dawned on me that what I looked for in answered prayer were highly selfish things: cessation of pain, a good job, healing, smooth interpersonal relationships, healthy finances. Rarely were my prayers concerned with bringing God glory. I had instead been hopeful that my life could be as painless as possible. But is that the purpose of prayer?

Jesus, our model for prayer, makes the purpose clear: Thinking of his coming crucifixion, he said, "Now my soul is deeply troubled. Should I pray, 'Father, save me from what lies ahead'? But that is the very reason why I came! Father, bring glory to your name" (John 12:27-28).

Upon studying the Scriptures, I discovered that the *real* purpose of prayer is not to obtain special blessings. It's to establish intimacy with God through regular communication with him. Without prayer, our relationship with God is one-sided; he communicates with us through his Word, but we don't return the favor. Certainly God knows our hopes and fears, our thoughts and feelings, before we tell him. But telling God these things changes our perspective.

Prayer is cooperation with God: not getting what I want, but learning what he wants.
ELISABETH ELLIOT GREN

How often do we pray as Christ did? How often do we say, "Father, bring glory to your name"?

God promises no hassle-free life for his people. In fact, he's most often glorified in times of suffering. God's greatest work was to do nothing while his Son died on a cross—despite the undoubtedly fervent prayers of Jesus' followers and Jesus' own Gethsemane prayer.

When I think of people whose deep Christian character and spiritual maturity have most influenced me, I think of people who have suffered. Why? Because in suffering, they've glorified God and grown profoundly in faith.

And that, I've discovered, is the purpose of prayer.

Joan L. Guest

A STEP FURTHER

Tips for Getting in Touch

1. *Take time to be quiet before God.* Don't pepper the Lord with requests; instead just listen. Even ten minutes spent alone can help you open yourself to God's Spirit.

2. *Pray through the Scriptures.* Read a short section and then stop. Listen to God. Talk to him about anything that strikes you in the passage. Let the Holy Spirit be your teacher.

3. *When you are especially busy, take a look at all the "little" things God provides for you each day:* air to breathe, beauty in nature, food to eat, smiles from others, laughter, songs and music. You'll never run out of things to glorify him for!

JLG

Faith Focus

What kind of things have you prayed for over the past week? Are your prayers self-oriented, emphasizing your own needs? Or do you thank God first for who he is and what he's done? What can you do to reflect Jesus' attitude today—and in the days to come—in your prayer life?

Prayer Pointer

Ask God to help you "bring glory to his name" in all you do—including your prayer life. Thank him for listening to your prayers, even when you don't know what to pray for or how to pray.

I AM THE TRUE VINE, AND MY FATHER IS THE GARDENER. HE CUTS OFF EVERY BRANCH THAT DOESN'T PRODUCE FRUIT, AND HE PRUNES THE BRANCHES THAT DO BEAR FRUIT SO THEY WILL PRODUCE EVEN MORE. . . . REMAIN IN ME, AND I WILL REMAIN IN YOU. FOR A BRANCH CANNOT PRODUCE FRUIT IF IT IS SEVERED FROM THE VINE, AND YOU CANNOT BE FRUITFUL APART FROM ME.

JOHN 15:1-2, 4

*H*ave you ever experienced a "dry spell"—
a time when your faith felt dull and circumstances in your life seemed uncertain?

As a forty-year-old single with limited
funds and a zeal for mission work, my friend
Janice had to move seven times in a year. But
through all the moves, Janice clung to John
15, knowing that God was at work in her life.
Now she's feeding and clothing homeless persons, using her own time of rootlessness to
reach them for Christ.

So if you're in a dry spell now, take heart.
God may be preparing you to be even more
fruitful in the days ahead!

How Does Your Garden Grow?

The azalea bush in my garden was struggling. Colorless leaves hung on limp branches with sparse flowers. I tenderly cut back every branch, assuring myself how lopping off lifeless branches would pave the way for new flowers next spring.

Suddenly, I realized how lovingly and gingerly God removes old branches from my life so I can sprout new growth. I wasn't punishing the azalea because it hadn't yielded enough flowers; I was doing everything I could to help it grow because I'm fond of the little bush and want it to do well. In the same way, God trims our life to help us improve because he loves us and wants to perfect us (Heb. 12:10-11).

If I weeded every day, it would take ten minutes. But when I say, "Those weeds aren't so bad. I'll get them tomorrow," I wind up spending an entire afternoon on my knees in the flower bed. So I've established the practice of getting rid of my weeds every day by recognizing the sins I've already committed and confessing them to God, who "is faithful and just and will forgive us our sins" (1 John 1:9, NIV).

We all have seasons when our walk with God isn't as fresh as it has been. But we can keep a dry spell from becoming a drought with regular prayer, Bible reading, and meaningful relationships with other Christians.

Ironically, it's during the dry spells we're most tempted to stop praying or reading the Bible. But that's when a garden needs water more than ever, and we need to receive encouragement by soaking up the rain God's already given us through his Word, his Spirit, his communion, and his people.

God is the perfect gardener. God doesn't wonder how to care for us; he created us and calls us by name (Isa. 43:1). God never leaves a flower bed half-weeded, but finishes the good work he started in us (Phil. 1:6). God waters us when we're thirsty (John 4:14) and feeds us when we're hungry (John 6:35). God gives us the faith to fight off the pests that would eat our fruit and stunt our growth (Eph. 6:16). When we fail to take advantage of his pesticides, he even restores what the locusts have eaten (Joel 2:25).

Once we commit our lives to the Lord and give him permission to come in and take over, he puts us in places where we have to grow to survive—and to realize our potential.
Susan Baker

In John 15 Jesus says he's the true vine and God's the gardener. We're the branches the gardener's grafted onto the true vine. Our only responsibility is to stay put and respond to the gardener. He'll till the ground, prune the old growth, send the rain and, ultimately, inhale the sweet aroma of the flowers if we'll cling to the true vine and grow.

How much simpler and richer life would be if we'd stop trying to create our own rain or plant our own seeds and cling instead to the true vine and its only gardener with all our heart, soul, and mind!   *Susan M. Smith*

A STEP FURTHER

Tending Your Inner Garden

1. *Allow God to pull the weeds in your life.*
   The sooner you let him, the smaller
   they'll be and easier to pull up!
2. *Evaluate how you handle the rainy days.*
   Do you use tough times to grow as a
   Christian—or to complain?
3. *Fertilize your spiritual growth.* Read God's
   Word and spend time with Christians
   who'll hold you accountable.
4. *Treat God as the ultimate gardener.* The
   old slogan "Let go and let God" is both
   easier—and more difficult—than you
   might think. But when we let God take
   over our self-gardens, he promises we'll
   get a bumper crop of righteousness!

SMS

Faith Focus

How are you growing as a Christian—through changing some habit or attitude, by becoming more disciplined in reading your Bible, or by growing more confident in telling others about Jesus? Are there areas in which you know God is pruning you: maybe in wasting too much time watching TV or in thinking unkind thoughts about your neighbor?

Prayer Pointer

Praise God today for three specific ways he's helping you grow. Thank him for the pruning process— even when it's not easy—and for what you're learning about yourself and him. Ask him to hold you accountable for continued growth.

WE KNOW THAT GOD CAUSES
EVERYTHING TO WORK TOGETHER
FOR THE GOOD OF THOSE WHO
LOVE GOD AND ARE CALLED AC-
CORDING TO HIS PURPOSE FOR
THEM. FOR GOD KNEW HIS PEOPLE
IN ADVANCE, AND HE CHOSE
THEM TO BECOME LIKE HIS SON.

ROMANS 8:28-29

DAY 3

*I*f you could delete any moment of your past, what moment would that be? The time you tripped over a chair and broke your wrist? The night a friend was critically injured in a car crash? The embarrassment you felt when your sibling picked a fight with you in front of your relatives?

We've all experienced moments we'd rather not relive. But according to Romans 8:28-29, even the worst times have a purpose: God can turn them into something good, for his glory.

If you ever wished you could undo your past, here's a fresh way to look at life's tough times.

Looking Back

There's a sign above my computer desk: "To err is human, but to really foul things up takes a computer." Yet despite the frustration my computer occasionally causes me, there's one thing about it I cherish—its "delete" key. What a wonderful little gizmo! With one press of a button it completely erases an unwanted document.

Yesterday I wished I could press some kind of delete key and undo a bit of my life. I'd erase the ten minutes of major hail that fell and caused our bathroom skylight to leak—again. Oh, and I'd abolish the thirty minutes I spent toiling at my desk while the spaghetti sauce I put on low boiled over on the stovetop and the rug.

But that's minor stuff. I'd love to do away with some major events in my life: the time my mother almost died following surgery; my rocky college relationship with then-boyfriend and now-husband, Jack; my sister's two years of suffering with leukemia.

Yet, wait—would I really want to delete those times?

I remember one morning, when my prayers for Jack's and my relationship seemed to hit the ceiling and bounce back, that I begged God to show me why my pleas for direction were going nowhere. He answered by showing me that Jack had become the most important person in my life—and that God would have no rival. I tearfully told the Lord I didn't want anyone to take his place in my life, that if he wanted me to be single, I'd trust him to know what was best. The peace I then experienced was beyond description.

Then there were early ministry years, when Jack and I literally had to trust the Lord for each day's food. Scary, no doubt about it. But then I recall the twenty dollars in our mailbox from an anonymous giver, the bag of groceries left on our back porch. God showed us his faithfulness in concrete ways. On second thought, I couldn't erase those days of need without obliterating God's provision!

And then there was the troubling time when my mother was ill and the painful two-year period when my sister Joye was dying, when God wrapped his arms around us and comforted us. There was the love extended by friends and by the body of Christ, the deep ways God revealed himself and the lessons he taught us, the closeness that bound our families together and remains today. And I reflect on my own changing view of heaven—how precious, real, wonderful it is to me because of those events.

Taking time out to remember the past—in all its sorrow and joy—is crucial. For reliving our memories is like looking through a window and seeing life's pieces fitting together in glory.
RAMONA CRAMER TUCKER

Even if I could, would I dare purge the events that seem horrible and unfair? Would I erase the deeper lessons that pain, suffering, frustration, sorrow—and yes, even death—bring? Can I not trust God with those events that still make no sense to me?

Now that I've given it serious thought, I'm still glad I have a delete key on my computer. But I'm even more glad that God, in his wisdom, didn't put one in my life.

Carole Mayhall

17

A Step Further

Gifts You Can Give Yourself in Tough Times

1. *The gift of time*. When life is overwhelming, take a walk, listen to an upbeat tape, relax with a cup of tea.
2. *The gift of empathy*. Gve yourself a break! Don't dwell on your failures; instead, move ahead.
3. *The gift of friendship*. Develop a caring "community" to encourage and support you through life's transitions.
4. *The gift of perspective*. Talk with someone you trust—a church leader, a counselor, or a mature friend.
5. *The gift of salvation*. Make sure your faith and trust are solidly on the only trustworthy person—Jesus Christ, who died for your sake.
6. *The gift of hope*. Study the topic of hope. Read about Jesus' miracles on earth and God's promises of healing and joy in heaven. RCT

Faith Focus

Have there been moments in the past year, whether minor or major, when *you* wished for a delete key? What made those situations so painful for you? What have you learned in the aftermath of those experiences? In what ways can you use tough times to grow as a Christian and also point others to heaven?

Prayer Pointer

Thank God for his omniscient power—and for his promise to work out all things together for good. Praise him for the ways he's currently working in your life, even when you sometimes don't understand the whys.

Don't be afraid, for I am with you. Do not be dismayed, for I am your God. I will strengthen you. I will help you. I will uphold you with my victorious right hand.

Isaiah 41:10

*O*K, I admit it. There are some things I'm afraid of—snakes, for one. Although I know they are God's creatures too, I can't seem to shake my childhood memory of meeting a rattlesnake the hard way—wrapped around the pole of my backyard swing set.

When fearful things happen, we could, like Maria in the *Sound of Music*, simply remember our favorite things and then we wouldn't feel so bad. But such a solution is short-term and simplistic.

The real solution to overcoming fear is claiming God's promises, such as Isaiah 41:10, and praising him.

Facing Fear Head-On

A jagged flash of lightning ripped open the night sky, and I sucked in my breath, instinctively hunching in fearful anticipation. A few seconds later, angry thunder vibrated across my nerves. I really hate lightning and thunder!

A room full of out-of-town relatives chuckled indulgently at my involuntary gasps each time lightning stabbed the sky, knowing well my fear of thunderstorms. But just as the storm seemed to pass, an earth-shattering crash snapped everyone to attention. The whole house shuddered.

"Whew! Lightning must have struck close," my uncle stated. "I'm going to look around." He opened the front door and took a step outside. "There's a fire!" he hollered.

I hurried outside to see flames leaping up a large juniper tree in the field across from our house, the orange glow growing with breathtaking speed.

"It's coming this way! We have to get out of here!" At the urgency in my uncle's voice, I raced for the phone, forcing my trembling fingers to punch the 911 buttons. Then I flew through the house, grabbing pictures off walls and photo albums from bookshelves. Within minutes everyone piled into the car, and as we drove down the driveway, I heard sirens. Help was on the way.

Later, the fire extinguished and our house safe, I drew two conclusions from that experience. My fear of thunderstorms wasn't so unreasonable, and fear only seems unreasonable when it's directed toward something you personally do not fear.

It's no fun to be afraid, but I'm glad God understands. The Bible is heavily laced with reassuring passages addressing fear. One of my favorites is about King Jehoshaphat, who had a legitimate reason to be afraid (2 Chron. 20). Three different armies had declared war on him. His solution? After praying for God's intervention, he had a choir lead his army into battle. As the choir sang praises to God, the three armies fought each other in a far-off valley. By the time Jehoshaphat's army arrived, no one was left to fight. All because of praise!

If we don't know what God is really like, if we have not worshiped in his presence, if we have not filled ourselves with his Word, then how can we possibly recognize God's presence in our lives?

LAURETTA PATTERSON

I gave Jehoshaphat's solution a try when my car broke down on the freeway late one night. Swallowing back my fear, I prayed, "Father, whatever happens now, I'll praise you—and I'll trust you."

Immediately a dark van lumbered to a stop and a powerfully built man stepped out and walked toward my car. I repeated, "I praise you, God, and I trust you."

As it turned out, the man was from the next town and knew which mechanic to recommend and tow company to call. In no time at all, I was back on the road. As I thanked the stranger for his help, he explained why he'd stopped. "Last week my wife's car broke down, and no one stopped to help her. I told the Lord the next time I passed a car on the side of the road, I'd stop."

Amazing! I'll remember this praise connection the next time I see storm clouds gathering.   *Mayo Mathers*

A STEP FURTHER

Fear Fighters

1. *Praise God for who he is.* God is Creator, Judge, Savior, Redeemer, and Holy One. He can handle any trouble you have!
2. *Praise God for what he's done throughout history.* Thank him for the miracles recorded in the Bible (the Israelites crossing the sea on dry ground, the feeding of the five thousand) and for his promise to care for you.
3. *Praise God for what he's done in your family's life.* Include situations he's used for good, family members who've come to Christ.
4. *Praise God for what he's currently doing in your life.* Thank him for your work, your home, and the opportunity to share Christ.
5. *Praise God for what he'll be doing in the future.* Thank him for working through you and giving you the promise of heaven as a free gift!   RCT

Faith Focus

What do you fear most? Losing your job or spouse? Facing the man who abused you? Not meeting this month's rent? What steps can you take today to actively turn those fears and concerns over to God?

Will you trust him enough to let him "strengthen you" and "help you," as Isaiah promises he will?

Prayer Pointer

Ask God, the one who has already overcome fear and death by dying on the cross for you and rising from the dead, to help you put your fears into an eternal perspective. Then thank him in advance for strengthening you and helping you the next time fear strikes.

Jesus told him, "I am the way, the truth, and the life. No one can come to the Father except through me. If you had known who I am, then you would have known who my Father is."

John 14:6-7

*A*ngel-on-your-shoulder pins. Television shows about priests and nuns. Crystals. Meditation. Classes that "open up your mind." Name-it, claim-it preachers. Cross necklaces. Our world today is filled with symbols of "spirituality." The word itself has a wide range of meaning that shows up everywhere, from books to screenplays, from sermons to songs, from advertisements to products.

But what does spirituality really mean? Is it Christian, or is it not? And how can we sort out what's godly from what's a whitewashing of God's truth? We need a way to tell the truth from the lies.

What's Wrong with "Spirituality"?

One day I heard the glorious strains of "Amazing Grace" coming from my TV set in the den. I ran to see who sang with such power the words "Amazing grace, how sweet the sound that saved a wretch like me!" After the song ended, the show's host complimented the soloist, a well-known recording artist, on her performance and asked, "Does that mean you've got religion in your life now?" I waited, eager to hear a wonderful story of conversion to Jesus Christ.

Instead the singer replied, "Of course not. Religion is what you get when you're afraid of hell. Spirituality is what you get when you've been there and back." I couldn't believe it! Although she'd sung the whole story of Christ's atoning work, to her, being saved meant she'd been rescued from the lostness of "not knowing who I was." Being "born again" meant getting in touch with her "inner self."

In the past I'd examined *spiritual* claims by comparing them to Scripture. But I'd never thought to see what the Bible said about spirituality. Oddly enough, when I did a search through my online Bible, the word *spirituality* wasn't found. Then I tried *spiritual* and all sorts of verses popped up. My friend Barb pointed out that throughout Scripture, *spiritual* is used to describe something else (i.e., spiritual gifts, spiritual truths). Spirituality, on the other hand, is something all by itself. Why is that an important distinction?

The Bible tells us our spiritual nature is dead in sin until we're born again by the Spirit of God who gives us spiritual birth through faith in Jesus Christ (John 3; Eph. 2:1-9). Any discussion of what it means to be "spiritual" must relate to that diagnosis of our condition. To become a Christian means we receive a person, Jesus—not a thing, spirituality.

And that means dealing with the specific claims Jesus made about himself—including his assertion that he is God—and facing the question "Are they true or not?"

Discovering truth about yourself and about God may feel at times like pulling an oar through molasses. But while you "row and pray," remember that an unseen Counselor is in the boat, and he is your way to shore.

KELSEY MENEHAN

The answer to who Jesus is marks the ultimate dividing line between who or what is and isn't Christian. Many religions and various forms of spirituality accept Jesus as a historical figure but reject him as the Christ, the one whom God sent to be "an atoning sacrifice for our sins" (1 John 4:10, NIV). Others talk of a "Christ-consciousness" in some mystical, global sense but refuse to tie that down to the flesh-and-blood person of Jesus Christ, the Son of God. The fact is, if a person has strong morals and values but doesn't embrace Jesus Christ as the only begotten Son of God, Savior, and resurrected Lord, his or her spirituality isn't Christian and cannot save.

Yet we need not fear today's spiritual confusion. As the darkness of false spirituality grows deeper, the light of God's truth can only shine brighter—pointing the way for those who still seek him. **Ruth E. Van Reken**

A Step Further

Is It Christian or Not?

1. *Logically examine what's being said.* Many statements about spirituality being passed off as "truth" today are not only lies, they're logically impossible.

2. *Compare popular spiritual concepts with what the Bible says.* For instance, Scripture says that Jesus (not angels or anyone else) is the mediator between God and man.

3. *Remember: Having a "Christian" label doesn't mean something is.* Just like the bank teller who knows the feel of counterfeit money after years of handling the real thing, our best protection against deception is to study and know God's revealed truth, the Bible.

4. *When someone speaks of spirituality, ask him or her to explain who Jesus is.* The answer to that question clearly divides who or what is and isn't Christian. REVR

Faith Focus

How will you respond to the concept of *spirituality* the next time you're

- talking with a friend or acquaintance?
- listening to a song or television program?
- considering a potential purchase?

In what ways can you shine as a beacon of God's truth to those around you?

Prayer Pointer

Ask God to give you an eager heart to investigate his Word, the discernment to tell right from wrong, and the ability to clearly reveal to others the truth about Jesus being the only way to God—and eternal life.

Never pay back evil for evil to anyone. Do things in such a way that everyone can see you are honorable. Do your part to live in peace with everyone, as much as possible. Dear friends, never avenge yourselves. Leave that to God. For it is written, "I will take vengeance; I will repay those who deserve it," says the Lord.

ROMANS 12:17-19

*L*ife isn't always fair. But why does it make us so angry when the bad guys seem to win? Maybe you've worked late for weeks, but a coworker steals the credit. Or your child loses his place on the basketball court to the school bully.

In times like those, it's hard to get down on our knees and "do [our] part to live in peace." But verses like Romans 12:17-19 are clear: We must leave any vengeance to God, even when we're fighting mad over life's injustices.

When Good Things Happen to Bad People

Sometimes when I read the newspaper, I'm outraged. A pastor and his wife lose six children in a fiery car crash. Lawyers gain wealth and fame from a televised trial. A child is wrested from loving Christian adoptive parents to be returned to birthparents who are virtual strangers. Whiny, spoiled athletes sign million-dollar contracts.

I can't figure out why people who seem to live only for their selfish pleasures become multimillionaires—while some of my most faithful Christian friends live one paycheck away from homelessness. I'm confounded when people who engage in shady business practices never get caught—they only get richer—and when people who lie and lust and gossip seem to go on their merry way.

Life isn't fair. I know bad things happen to good people. But it really bothers me when good things happen to bad people—or at least people who don't seem especially worthy.

It's easy to wonder, *Where's the payoff? Does God even notice if I'm trying to be good?* Some aspects of the Christian faith seem so contrary to human nature. We know it's wrong to begrudge others their good fortune, so what should our response be? How can we rise above the trap of envy, resentment, or scorekeeping?

When I asked one of my friends for her perspective on this question, she responded laughingly, "Boy, I have enough trouble worrying about myself! I'm so far off the mark, I can't even bother to think about whether others deserve what they get."

When I read my Bible, here's the message I get: Because I've been saved by grace—meaning unmerited favor—my primary task is to become more Christlike through the work of his Spirit in me. As one of God's adopted children, he holds me to a higher standard, and it's a daily, humbling challenge to live up to that standard. As Oswald Chambers observed, "Never waste your time looking for justice; if you do, you will soon put yourself in bandages and give way to self-pity. Our business is to see that no one suffers from our injustice."

It's often when I'm feeling proud of myself, thinking, *Hey, God, look at me! What a good servant I am,* that God shoots off some reminder of my foolishness and dependence on him. When I'm tempted to think of myself as worthy, Romans 3:23 provides a pithy corrective: All have sinned. None is "worthy" except God alone. And whenever I whine about the good fortune undeserving people seem to be blessed with while I muddle along, I'm being less like Christ.

If we want to wrestle through the injustices of life, we must realize God is all-mighty. He's able to use even the treachery of others for his own good.
PATSY CLAIRMONT

Above all, it's good to remember I don't really know the state of a life or a soul. That's God's business. So now, instead of being depressed about the injustices I read about in the newspaper or encounter in everyday life, I try to thank God for what I have—including good friends, food to share with them, a modest home, and most of all, the reassurance that God is with me always.

And that's enough. More than enough.
Elizabeth Cody Newenhuyse

A Step Further

Survival Strategies for Unfair Times

1. *Think before you judge.* Appearances can deceive, causing us to hastily type people as "good" or "bad." But we don't always know what's going on inside a person— or inside that home we admire.
2. *Trust God's justice.* Tragedy happens. The bad guys sometimes win. The world is not just, but God is. And God will deal with the wicked (Rom. 12:19).
3. *Remember what matters.* When we speak of "good things" happening to bad people, we often mean worldly success. But God's blessings sometimes sidestep the obvious.
4. *Remember who matters.* The final, most important step we can take is to express our gratitude for God himself, to share our feelings of love, humility, and wonder.

ECN

Faith Focus

Have you ever fallen into the trap of envy, resentment, or scorekeeping? If so, how have you felt afterward? Did it help—or hinder—your spiritual growth? In what ways can you focus on blessings instead?

Prayer Pointer

Ask the Lord to help you focus on the many blessings he's given you—including family, friends, material possessions, and most of all, what he has done for your soul. Thank him specifically for each treasure and for the hope of eternal life with him.

You should behave . . . like God's very own children, adopted into his family—calling him "Father, dear Father." For his Holy Spirit speaks to us deep in our hearts and tells us that we are God's children. And since we are his children, we will share his treasures—for everything God gives to his Son, Christ, is ours, too.

Romans 8:15-17

*W*hat do you know about your dad? His height and weight? His personality? Where he was born, and the places he's lived? His spiritual beliefs? If you had to write an obituary after his death, what would you say?

Some of us may know the answers to those questions; others may have had little or no contact with their father. But whether your father was present or absent when you were growing up, we all yearn for a father's love.

One of the best ways to meet that longing—forever—is to get to know your heavenly Father, who treats you as his child (Rom. 8:15-17) and will never leave you.

How Well Do You Know Your Father?

Our local newspaper was sponsoring an essay contest, "Why My Father Is the Best," and since I was teaching a high-school writing class, that was the assignment I gave. All students but one were busily writing. Julie stared at the wall as her pen rolled off her desk and clattered to the floor.

"Need some ideas to get started, Julie?" I prodded.

"I'm not doing this assignment!" she stated flatly. "My dad's dead."

"Is there another man you could write about then? A grandfather, maybe, or an uncle or stepfather?"

"I've had four stepfathers, and they all abused me. Now my mom's new boyfriend has moved in with us." The venom in her voice made me shiver.

Not knowing how to respond, I silently pleaded with the Lord for help. "Julie," I whispered, kneeling beside her desk so only she could hear me, "just because your father's dead doesn't mean you can't write about him. Pretend he's here right now. What would you tell him?"

She studied me for a few moments, then nodded. For the rest of the class, her pen scratched furiously across page after page of notebook paper. When the bell rang, Julie brought her essay to me.

"May I read it to you?" she asked quietly.

What she read was a profoundly intimate love letter from a daughter to her father. She ended by saying, "Though you died before I could know you, you are the best father in the world. I love you, Daddy."

I've never forgotten that conversation with Julie. I, too, knew what it was like to grow up without a dad, but I never had to endure a parade of men through my home. In fact, I was so young when he died, and my mother was such a positive force in my life, that I honestly didn't feel bad about not having a father.

It wasn't until the birth of my own sons that I realized what I'd missed. One afternoon my husband, Steve, swept Tyler up in a huge bear hug and swung him around in his arms while Tyler squealed in delight.

So that's what I missed! I thought as unexpected, jagged grief brought tears to my eyes. It was then, nearly twenty years after his death, that I began to grieve for my father. For some time I floundered in the world of "what might have been." The most often repeated phrase in my mind became *If only I'd had a father.* Then Romans 8:15-17 brought my self-pity to an abrupt halt. It said we've been adopted into God's family and that we can call him "Father"—for we really are his children.

> *When you spend time with God, he gives you a deep sense of knowing you've been with him.*
> SUSAN HOWARD

Those familiar words suddenly became rich with new meaning. I had a father! And he would never leave me, not through death, divorce, abuse, or abandonment . . . not ever! I smiled heavenward as the security of those words wrapped around me in a warm hug.

Now, on Father's Day and every day, I have a heavenly Father to celebrate.   *Mayo Mathers*

A STEP FURTHER

Longing for a Father?

1. *Search through Scripture for references to God as Father.* Here's a start: Matthew 18:19; John 14:2, 6; 2 Corinthians 1:3-4; 2 John 1:2-3.
2. *Get to know older, godly couples* who can provide the mature wisdom and friendship you're longing for.
3. *Read books by Christian fathers,* such as Ken Canfield, Dr. James Dobson, etc. And don't forget to look at what Scripture says about being a dad (see Prov. 1:8-9; Eph. 6:4; 1 Tim. 3:1-5).
4. *Ask God to fill your father-longing with "children."* These may be younger believers you can parent in the faith or disadvantaged children who themselves don't have a dad.

RCT

Faith Focus

How well do you know your heavenly Father? What steps can you take to get to know him better so that you can call him "Abba" (Daddy) in loving trust?

Prayer Pointer

Praise God today for being your heavenly Father. Thank him for offering you eternal security in his arms. Ask him to fill your father-relationship needs in his way, in his time, and for his glory.

Jesus told them, "I assure you, even if you had faith as small as a mustard seed you could say to this mountain, 'Move from here to there,' and it would move. Nothing would be impossible."

MATTHEW 17:20

DAY 8

*C*hristian history is full of folks who doubted God but didn't lose their faith. Take "doubting" Thomas, for example. Although he had heard Jesus predict his death and resurrection, he still didn't believe the other disciples when they said that Jesus had appeared to them. "Not until I touch his wounds will I believe," Thomas said.

So Jesus showed up and let Thomas do exactly that. You see, Jesus knows that we, as human beings, sometimes doubt God's power to work in our life—and that we need help to improve our spiritual vision.

Dealing with Doubt

I have a confession to make: I have lots of doubts. I doubt airline operators who tell me the plane is "on time." I doubt bookkeeping departments who say, "The check is in the mail."

But I have bigger doubts than these, and sometimes they worry me. Sometimes I doubt God. From time to time, I wonder about God's control of this world, which seems bent on destruction. Or I question his involvement in my life. Can God change circumstances? Will he? Is he really intimately involved in the day-to-day?

I know I'm not the only Christian to struggle with doubt, yet often there's a conspiracy of silence in Christian circles about doubting. Doubt is something to be avoided, squelched, or uprooted, but certainly not acknowledged or embraced. When a friend, shattered by one too many disappointments, told me recently, "For the next few weeks I'm giving myself permission to question God's love," I felt myself gasp inwardly. Can she really do that? Won't she lose her faith?

There seems to be a biblical basis for being frightened by doubt. The apostle James wrote that "a doubtful mind is as unsettled as a wave of the sea that is driven and tossed by the wind. People like that should not expect to receive anything from the Lord" (James 1:6-7). It's that state of limbo that must have prompted one Christ follower to blurt out in confused exasperation, "I believe! Help my unbelief!"

Many of our doubts grow out of a distorted picture of God. God can and does intervene in our daily life, but his purposes are much grander than we can imagine. The Old

Testament patriarch Job thought he knew God. Certainly he knew more about God's character than his supposed "friends" who came to tell him why he was suffering so much. But even this man we think of as a paragon of faith reached the point when self-pity and doubt nearly overwhelmed his belief in God.

In trying to explain his suffering, Job begins to accuse God. God replies forcefully, "Where were you when I laid the foundations of the earth?" (Job 38:4)—and proceeds to speak of the wonders of his creation. In this exchange, Job's eyes are opened to see God in a new way. "I was talking about things I did not understand, things far too wonderful for me," Job says. "I had heard about you before, but now I have seen you with my own eyes" (Job 42:3, 5).

Whenever I have to make a decision, it's wonderful to know that when I ask for wisdom, God will give it liberally—if only I have faith to accept it.
LEANZA CORNETT

And so it is with us. We see God through a human lens—a very cloudy one at that. But through praying, studying Scripture, and looking intently for God's face in our everyday life our spiritual vision can improve.

Today, when doubts sneak up on me, I remember that faith can sap energy from doubt just as easily as the other way around. As I bring to mind the many ways God has loved me with a perfect love over my lifetime, my frail faith is encouraged—and the cloud of doubt, once again, moves away. *Kelsey D. Menehan*

47

A Step Further

Remedies for Doubt

1. *Find the reason for your doubt.* Ask your-self why you're doubting God—is it to grow closer to him or because you don't want to do what he's asking you to do?
2. *Improve your vision.* Don't limit God's role in your life to merely Grand Fixer of Circumstances.
3. *Exercise what little faith you have.* "Doing" the Word of God activates faith and helps it grow. Our doubts may not disappear, but they'll begin to weigh less.
4. *Remember.* Keep a journal so you can see God's loving, faithful presence in your everyday life.
5. *Find a faith community.* Get involved in a church where you feel comfortable sharing your questions—and where you receive help and accountability.   KDM

Faith Focus

At what times have you most felt God's active presence? Was it in good times or difficult times? How can looking for those "touchstones" reaffirm your faith in the future when doubt looms large?

Prayer Pointer

Recall a "touchstone" from your life. Thank God for the way in which he worked in that particular moment to guide and guard your life or to help you make a big decision. Ask him to help you believe he's in control of the present and future, even when you doubt.

WORK HARD AND CHEERFULLY AT
WHATEVER YOU DO, AS THOUGH
YOU WERE WORKING FOR THE
LORD RATHER THAN FOR PEOPLE.
REMEMBER THAT THE LORD WILL
GIVE YOU AN INHERITANCE AS
YOUR REWARD, AND THE MASTER
YOU ARE SERVING IS CHRIST.

COLOSSIANS 3:23-24

*T*eaching a Sunday school class. Tutoring a student in reading. Helping a struggling ministry. Choosing to be a wife and full-time mom. Starting a home day-care business. Caring for an elderly parent.

There are all kinds of work we can do for God—whether it's up front or behind the scenes. Some think they're not serving God unless they're in a high-profile ministry. However, that's not what Colossians 3:23-24 says. God tells us that *whatever we do* for him is valuable. And caring for those in need is high on his priority list.

Are You a Behind-the-Scenes Christian?

A noise—undefined—wakes me, and I sit up quickly, rubbing my neck to relieve a kink from a restless night. Listening intently, I hear low moans coming from the next room. I spring from bed and hurry through the darkness.

My ninety-four-year-old mother-in-law sits on her bed, groaning. "I've got pains right here," she says, pointing under her rib cage.

When her pains don't subside, I call 911. Within six minutes, five men crowd the apartment, bundle up Mom, and with me riding in the front seat of the ambulance, rush to the emergency room.

Tests finally over, we settle at last in the sparse hospital room. I reflect on the last two and a half months and our first real brush with the intricacies of "elder care"—a time that has been all-consuming emotionally, mentally, and physically for our family. Recently the lion's share has fallen on my husband, Jack, and me as we live with Mom in her California apartment. I realize I have much to learn about "pure religion," as described in James 1:27: "Pure and lasting religion in the sight of God our Father means that we must care for orphans and widows in their troubles, and refuse to let the world corrupt us."

The first definition concerns external deeds; the second, internal life. However, they share a common denominator: Both are done behind the scenes. Neither is in-your-face, up-front, or public. Instead, it's that almost invisible obedience on which God places a high premium.

My time with Mom cleared my thinking regarding various assignments God gives his children. For instance, a friend who's immersed in speaking and counseling is frequently frazzled. But my heart swells with admiration for her dedication—and rightly so. Another woman I know works hard at a fulfilling career and arrives home bushed. I respect her passion—and rightly so. My grown daughter is worn-out some days from caring for two teenagers, participating in her husband's ministry, and balancing home with a part-time job. I understand, sympathize, and admire her—and rightly so.

> *The thing I love about being a Christian is that the ground is level at the foot of the cross. God equips all of us for service.*
> JILL BRISCOE

But in the past, I'd felt sorry for my friend Pat, whose elderly mother is in a nearby care facility. Pat's time is consumed with visits, telephone calls, and meeting her mom's needs. There are days when she's absolutely exhausted. Yet somehow I viewed Pat's fatigue—from caring for a "widow or orphan"—as different from the others. I unconsciously viewed the care of others the way the world does—as an imposition, an inconvenience, or an interruption.

Now I'm convinced God views serving others as not only important but imperative. And I think God's going to reserve his greatest smile for me not for leading a Bible study, but for reading aloud to one whose eyes are failing. Not for handing out advice, but for handing out medication. Not for preparing a lavish meal for guests, but for preparing three small meals for an even smaller appetite. *Carole Mayhall*

A Step Further

Caring for Older Folks

1. *Write a monthly note of encouragement.*
   Older people, especially those in nursing
   homes, love to get regular mail.
2. *Regularly visit an older person who lives
   alone.* Bring in clippings of news items
   and her favorite snack food. Then be
   prepared to talk—and listen! The
   elderly have decades of wonderful
   stories to tell.
3. *Volunteer to drive.* Whether it's to the
   grocery store, to the doctor's office,
   or to church each Sunday, your offer
   will be appreciated.
4. *Give a hand to Meals on Wheels.* Or start
   your own service from your own kitchen!
5. *Volunteer one morning a week at the local
   senior citizens center.* Share your talent
   for crafts, music, or letter writing, along
   with the good news of Jesus Christ.   CM

Faith Focus

How much time do you spend in behind-the-scenes caring for others? The next time you're called upon to care for someone, how will you respond? Will you do it because you have to? or so others will admire your "selfless sacrifice"? or because you love God and want to obey him?

Prayer Pointer

Pray, asking the Lord to help you as you honestly evaluate your commitment to caring for others. Then ask him to reveal to you what "good works" you should be doing for him and what items need to be sacrificed in your schedule to fulfill *his* priorities for your life.

We loved you so much that we gave you not only God's Good News but our own lives, too. Don't you remember, dear brothers and sisters, how hard we worked among you? . . . We pleaded with you, encouraged you, and urged you to live your lives in a way that God would consider worthy. For he called you into his Kingdom to share his glory.

1 Thessalonians 2:8-9, 12

*W*hen my new friend Michelle became a Christian, I was overjoyed. Because of her many past experiences with not-so-loving Christians, I knew her step toward God was truly one of faith. Now, four years later, although she's still in a difficult marriage, she faces life with a content, peaceful attitude. When others ask her how she came to the faith, she says, "All it took for me to want to be a Christian was one person who truly acted Christlike."

Witnessing isn't as risky or hard as we might think—and it can be fun too!

Spread the Word!

In 1981 I was as far away from righteous living as a woman could get. Then a husband-and-wife team who were new in Christ started working at the radio station where I was the host of the midday show.

This couple didn't know tons of Bible verses yet, but they knew Jesus Christ. They hadn't memorized the Four Spiritual Laws, but they knew how to care about people. Simply put, they invited me into their home, welcomed me into their lives, and loved me into the family of God.

Months later I followed their example and shared my limited but enthusiastic knowledge of the Lord with two work friends—with the same surprising result. I wrote their names in the margin of my Bible, right next to 1 Thessalonians 2:8: "We loved you so much that we were delighted to share with you not only the gospel of God but our lives as well, because you had become so dear to us" (NIV).

Many years and many changed lives later, I'm convinced that sharing your faith simply requires caring enough to let someone else know how Christ has changed your life.

For instance, I was on a late-evening trip to Detroit when a flight attendant strolled the aisle of our nearly empty plane and glanced over my shoulder at the book I was reading.

"What's that about?" she asked. I grinned. It was Rebecca Pippert's classic book on lifestyle evangelism, *Out of the Saltshaker*.

I showed her the cover and said, "It's about how to share your faith."

Her eyebrows went up. "Really?" In a casual, matter-of-fact way, I briefly shared my journey from a party-hearty lifestyle of drugs and promiscuity to a new life of joy and purpose in Christ.

Sitting down across the aisle from me, she said, "It's made that much of a difference for you, huh?"

At that moment, the pilot announced our approach to Detroit Metro Airport, and she jumped up to resume her duties. But before she headed up the aisle, I asked, "May I pray for you?" and she tearfully nodded yes.

Sometimes God calls us to be gentle in our witness; other times, to be bold. One spring day, the program director of my radio station called me into his office, excitement on his face. "Liz, we've got a great idea for your midday show. Every Thursday, you'll feature an hour of call-ins with a psychic. It's a great opportunity to increase your ratings!"

Being a missionary doesn't mean hitting people over the head with the gospel all the time. But it does mean we live our lives so others ask, "Hey, you're different. Why?"

KAY ARTHUR

Boldly saying no for the cause of Christ produced fruit in the months that followed. The ratings went up (without the psychic), and the program director became a Christian and married a precious sister in Christ. I love happy endings!

Sharing the gospel isn't so much what you know as whom you know. If you know the Savior and are surrounded by friends and family who haven't met him yet, then who better to handle the introductions than you?

Liz Curtis Higgs

A STEP FURTHER

Five Ways to Share God's Love

1. *Be there* (Rom. 12:15)—*and be an encourager* (Heb. 3:13). Is a coworker having a birthday? Have a card waiting on her desk. Is a friend struggling with two toddlers? Stop by with a bucket of chicken at dinnertime.
2. *Be generous with your resources.* Proverbs 22:9 says, "Blessed are those who are generous, because they feed the poor."
3. *Love, don't judge* (Matt. 7:1). It's the Holy Spirit's business, not ours, to convince people that they're sinners.
4. *Choose your words carefully.* Proverbs 25:11 declares, "Timely advice is as lovely as golden apples in a silver basket."
5. *Say you'll pray—then do it.* The apostle Paul wrote, "God knows how often I pray for you. Day and night I bring you and your needs in prayer to God" (Rom. 1:9). LCH

Faith Focus

When you think of sharing your faith, do you (1) break out in a cold sweat? or (2) smile in eager anticipation?

What gifts do you have that could help you love people into God's company?

Prayer Pointer

Thank God for the power of his Good News that can transform people's lives. Then ask him to give you opportunities, the courage to speak, and the right words for that particular situation. Pray specifically for one person's salvation over the next month.

NOW, JUST AS YOU ACCEPTED CHRIST JESUS AS YOUR LORD, YOU MUST CONTINUE TO LIVE IN OBEDIENCE TO HIM. LET YOUR ROOTS GROW DOWN INTO HIM AND DRAW UP NOURISHMENT FROM HIM, SO YOU WILL GROW IN FAITH, STRONG AND VIGOROUS IN THE TRUTH YOU WERE TAUGHT. LET YOUR LIVES OVERFLOW WITH THANKSGIVING FOR ALL HE HAS DONE.

COLOSSIANS 2:6-7

 Christian leader disappoints you. A friend gossips about you. You lose your job. Your heartfelt prayer for a spouse seems to go unheard.

Because we live in a sinful world, we all have life situations that shake our faith—and make us reevaluate what it means to be a child of God.

But it's in the tough circumstances, when we can't see the path ahead, that we must learn to do two things, according to Colossians 2:6-7: obey God and praise him for what he's already done. And in the process, we discover spiritual truths we can depend on.

Five Truths You Can Count On

In my teen years, I attended a church with a banner across the front of the sanctuary that read "Jesus Christ, the same yesterday, today, and forever." It's good to know some things in this universe never change.

But my faith did. As I grew up and dealt with life disappointments—family and career changes, financial difficulties, and what seemed like an eternal state of singlehood—the faith I'd been so sure of in my teens seemed up for grabs by my mid-twenties. Ultimately, my personal struggles forced me to reevaluate my beliefs.

Now in my late thirties, I trust even more strongly in these five foundational basics of Christianity that have stood the test of time and sustained generations of believers before me.

We're saved by grace, and we grow by grace. No matter how many years we've been in the faith, no matter how many wonderful things we've done or ministries we've been involved in, we're still completely dependent on the forgiveness, acceptance, and guidance of Christ in our life. Our growth into Christ's likeness results from our growing acknowledgment of God's work in us and our increasing dependence upon him. Grace is what makes good on our mistakes and setbacks.

God hears our prayers. God repeatedly proves he loves answering prayer. And he often grants blessings we didn't even think to pray for. As we grow in greater confidence of God's love, we become less concerned about his actual answers to the items on our prayer list and more certain that he indeed hears us and will respond to our requests out of perfect wisdom (see Ps. 34:17-18; Luke 18:1-8).

We're members of a body. You don't have to be a sociologist to see that God designed people for relationship. Although every church has some problems and weaknesses, our commitment to Christ needs to include a commitment to be connected to his people. Our potential for ministry broadens, too, when we don't try to go it alone, when we join a Bible-believing church that's committed to applying God's truth to daily life and working together to win others to the body of Christ (see 1 Cor. 12:12-31; Eph. 4:1-16).

> *I'm learning to let go and cast my cares on him,*
> *to be God-dependent instead of Jan-dependent.*
> JAN DRAVECKY

Real Christianity will cost you. It was Christ's servant heart and humility that took him to the cross. Why, then, are we surprised or irritated when Jesus tells us to deny ourselves and follow him? But as we face pains and losses for the sake of the Kingdom, God's grace in our lives increases, and so does our faith.

The results are up to God. Little by little, I'm learning to pray with my hands opened, palms upward, to symbolize that whatever I'm praying about I'm ultimately surrendering to God. Sometimes I give up those things only for a few moments before grabbing them back again. But I'm committed to practicing this attitude before God, to give God the opportunity to increase my faith and maturity.

Vinita Hampton Wright

A Step Further

Spiritual-Growth Checklist

1. *Cultivate good spiritual habits,* including reading your Bible, praying to God, and worshiping him individually and corporately.
2. *Depend on the Holy Spirit for help and guidance.*
3. *Pray*—individually and with friends, family, or your prayer group. There's strength in numbers. Jesus told his disciples, "For where two or three gather together because they are mine, I am there among them" (Matt. 18:20).
4. *Live by faith, not in fear.* See Hebrews 11 for a definition and examples of faith.
5. *Appreciate what you have.*
6. *Give up control. Give up worry*—and relax. The results are already in God's hands. You can be at peace.   VHW

Faith Focus

At what points in your life have you reevaluated your faith? And what were the results of those difficult times? What did you discover about God and about yourself? What particular truths will you hang on to when you face future struggles?

Prayer Pointer

Thank God for taking charge of the universe—and for proving repeatedly that nothing is too difficult for him to accomplish. Then ask him to give you courage and perseverance as you make your spiritual growth a priority.

Don't be afraid and don't worry. Instead, you must worship Christ as Lord of your life. And if you are asked about your Christian hope, always be ready to explain it.

1 Peter 3:14-15

*M*y friends Jill and Annie couldn't be more different. Jill is gentle and more reserved; Annie is outspoken and loves to generate lively discussions.

But they're also the best of friends because they share a common love: their passion for telling others how Christ has changed their life. Jill talks with her coworkers and neighbors over a cup of coffee. Annie goes door-to-door in her apartment complex, welcoming new renters with homemade cookies and a tract.

The Bible tells us we must "always be ready to explain" our faith. Why? Because being a Christian is a big deal—and we can't afford to let others miss out.

What's the Big Deal about Being a Christian?

Not long ago, my sister, Carole, called me long-distance to catch up—we talked about marriage, work, kids. Then our conversation shifted to the topic of faith.

"What's the big deal about being a Christian, anyway?" Carole asked me.

Her directness caught me off guard. Since our conversation, I've pondered her question. Although I always believed in God, it wasn't until I was twenty-three that I began asking questions like those Carole is now asking. I kept meeting people who had devoted their lives to serving the Lord, and their relationship with Jesus gave them a peace and power I found irresistible.

Seven years ago, I finally accepted Jesus as my Savior. As I looked back on my excursion from nominal believer to committed Christian—and the ways my life has changed—I came up with these reasons I'm glad I'm a Christian.

The gift of peace. While the promise of eternal life is central to our faith, knowing Jesus isn't something we only experience in the future. He's present in our lives now, enabling us to live according to his will. Recognizing God's provision for my needs reassures me of his presence and gives me a peace only he offers, despite the circumstances I experience in the world.

A clean slate. I'm constantly humbled by my own sinfulness. I'd assumed that once I had a personal relationship with Christ, I wouldn't struggle with gossiping or yelling at my family. While God has given me the strength to overcome some struggles, I have to ask for forgiveness every day for other failures. What a freedom it is to stand before him and admit my failures, then have my slate wiped clean every day!

Purpose for living. After struggling for years with the issue of significance, I've finally realized that if I shed all the roles I play, my ultimate job is to reflect the living Christ within me. This truth has given every job I do significance. Understanding God's will for us isn't always easy. But believing he's in charge and has a plan for us makes the journey worth traveling.

> *To grow in faith is a risky business, filled with trial and error, unknown challenges and experiences—and unimaginable rewards.*
> HARRIET CROSBY

Absolutes in an "anything goes" world. God's Word truly is "a lamp for my feet and a light for my path" (Ps. 119:105). Through Scripture God sets the standard by which we are to live. He spells out right from wrong, and I'm constantly accountable to him for my actions. If ever there was a how-to book on life, the Bible is it.

Hope in the midst of sadness. The first Christmas after my dad died was the loneliest holiday season of my life—but also one of the most meaningful. For the first time I realized how glad I was to be a Christian. As a believer, I can enjoy Christmas every day. Through the infant Jesus, I'm reminded of the hope for salvation and eternal life his presence in the world offered then—and today.   *Marian V. Liautaud*

A Step Further

Practicing Praise

1. *Thank God with your heart.* What God longs for most is your grateful heart.
2. *Thank God by obeying his commands in the Bible.* God is honored when we treat his Word as our life guide.
3. *Thank God by praising him for creating you, just as you are.* Every person has times when she doesn't like herself very much. But remembering that God made you as you are, for his glorious purposes, can transform such times into a godly thank-session!
4. *Thank God with your choices.* We say thank you to God for his wisdom every time we choose his way over Satan's way.
5. *Thank God by taking care of his creations.* This includes plants, animals, orphaned children, and hurting adults.   RCT

Faith Focus

If someone asked you right now, "What difference has Christ made in your life?" what would you say? What reasons would you give for why you're glad to be a Christian?

Prayer Pointer

Thank God for his gifts to you, including peace, a clean slate, purpose for living, absolutes in an "anything goes" world, and hope in the midst of sadness. Ask God to give you an opportunity to share one of those gifts with a friend, neighbor, or coworker.

THE LORD YOUR GOD HAS AR-
RIVED TO LIVE AMONG YOU. HE IS
A MIGHTY SAVIOR. HE WILL RE-
JOICE OVER YOU WITH GREAT
GLADNESS. WITH HIS LOVE, HE
WILL CALM ALL YOUR FEARS. HE
WILL EXULT OVER YOU BY SINGING
A HAPPY SONG.

ZEPHANIAH 3:17

*W*hen I first met my friend Brynna, she rarely cracked a smile and never got angry. Then one day she phoned me, sounding strangely excited. "You wouldn't believe what I found out today. It's OK to have emotions and to show them—because God does, too!" That discovery led to a changed life for Brynna. She learned that, just as God could show joy over her (Zeph. 3:17), she could rejoice in life, too. Now her sweet smiles attract others like honey.

If you or someone you know lives in the "emotional land of bland," this next devotion is just for you.

Experiencing God's Emotions

I grew up in a devoutly religious subculture, and it didn't take me long to figure out that the people it contained were not the most liberated, expressive folks in the world.

By the time I was six or seven, I'd already learned that raucous laughter needed to be toned down, that sorrow-filled people needed to mop up their tears. Angry people needed to back off if they knew what was good for them, and tender people needed to toughen up if they planned to survive in this world. It seemed as if all the genuine emotions that welled up first needed to pass through a spiritual filter, causing them to lose most of their punch before they were considered "Christian."

Many years later, well after I became a Christian, I found myself pondering, *Can Christians be joyful without running the risk of becoming frivolous or silly? How long can we feel sad before we become morose or faithless? Can we become angry without being accused of being unchristian? How tender can we be without becoming sentimental saps?*

It's possible to fall into the trap of thinking a life of carefully limited emotions is what pleases God most. But that often results in a tragic loss of vigor in individuals and in the family of God. Too many people spend too much time in the emotional land of bland.

Jesus perfectly reflected God's nature in every situation he encountered on earth (see John 5:19). When we look at his example, we discover a full range of feelings. Here are a few:

Jesus knew joy. One of the recurring phrases in his ministry was that we should obey his commands so "our joy might be made full." Whenever God sees people acting in ways that honor him, when he receives the right kind of worship, when he sees faith, the Bible says he's smiling with delight.

Jesus experienced soul-wrenching sorrow. He wept at the tomb of his friend Lazarus—and when he saw people wandering around like sheep without a shepherd, wrecking their lives. When Jesus prayed in Gethsemane before his impending crucifixion, he was overwhelmed with sorrow.

Jesus had the ability to be angry. When the money changers turned the temple into a corrupt casino-type atmosphere, Jesus grabbed some rope, made a whip, and cleared the place out to let everybody know his righteous outrage at what had happened to his place of worship. Anger is a legitimate response to the injustices in this world and to the other sins that break God's heart and violate his Word.

> *I have bad days and good days. But I can show joy in the midst of sorrow and peace that passes all understanding. That's what people are looking for.*
> CeCe Winans

Jesus felt tenderness. When he saw fragile people on the brink of despair, he treated them gently. Jesus didn't just greet kids; he held them tenderly on his lap. He wouldn't just call out for lepers to be healed; he'd embrace them. When we're in relationship with God, his love and gentleness will meet all our needs. And if our all-powerful God isn't threatened by being tender, we shouldn't be either! **Bill Hybels**

A Step Further

Getting out of the Land of Bland

1. *Rejoice with those who rejoice, and weep with those who weep* (Rom. 12:15).
2. *Investigate God's emotions through Scripture:*
   - Joy—Genesis 1
   - Sorrow—Matthew 26:38; Psalm 56:8
   - Tenderness—Isaiah 42:3
   - Anger—Hebrews 10:26-27
3. *Check your emotional responses against Scripture.* For instance, are you angry for selfish reasons (because you lost out) or because someone/something has hurt the cause of Christ?
4. *Ask God to help you respond with his emotions*—at the appropriate time, in the appropriate place.

BH

Faith Focus

A bumper sticker I once saw read "There are two types of people—those who blow their stack and those who stuff everything in a sack." What about you? Do you show your emotions easily (maybe *too* easily at times)? Or do you have difficulty showing even the "righteous" emotions because you fear someone might think you're a sap or a hothead?

How can you more accurately reflect who God is to the watching world through expressing your emotions in a Christlike manner?

Prayer Pointer

Praise God for his creativity in giving you a range of emotions. Thank him for joy and tenderness, and yes, even sorrow and anger. Ask him to help you sort right from wrong motives and to give you the confidence and freedom to express your emotions when and where it's appropriate.

EVERY TIME I THINK OF YOU, I GIVE THANKS TO MY GOD. I ALWAYS PRAY FOR YOU, AND I MAKE MY REQUESTS WITH A HEART FULL OF JOY. . . . AND I AM SURE THAT GOD, WHO BEGAN THE GOOD WORK WITHIN YOU, WILL CONTINUE HIS WORK UNTIL IT IS FINALLY FINISHED ON THAT DAY WHEN CHRIST JESUS COMES BACK AGAIN.

PHILIPPIANS 1:3-4, 6

I'll pray for you." How often I've said these words to friends, neighbors, coworkers, and family. Although I earnestly mean them when I say them, sometimes I don't follow through. I get sidetracked by life's details and busyness—or I just plain forget.

But God tells us that praying for others is not an option—it's part of obeying him! As Philippians 1:3-4, 6 says, we should *think of*, *pray for*, and *thank God for* others. And we can choose to do all this with joy and anticipation, knowing that it's a privilege.

Praying for Others

Just after our second anniversary, my husband and I closed the deal on our first home. It was a huge step for both of us, but much prayer and a series of events clearly orchestrated by God confirmed our decision. Then eight months later our income was cut in half when my job ended unexpectedly. Although we knew God would provide for our needs, the possibility of losing our new home seemed overwhelming.

When we shared our concern with others, we encountered a plethora of "solutions." Very few said what we most wanted to hear: "I'll be praying for you."

In this age of instant pudding, instant cameras, and instant credit, people seem compelled to find an instant solution to every problem. But most people don't expect their friends to solve their problems—they simply want them to care enough to pray.

Intercessory prayer isn't as complicated as it may seem. Next time a friend has a problem, don't fall into the trap of simply offering advice or allowing your fears to keep you from accepting the responsibility and privilege of praying for her. Here are a few pointers to get you started:

Be sincere. "I'll pray for you" glides off our tongue so smoothly—but the promise is worthless if it's not backed up with action. We need to be cautious about casually committing ourselves to pray for someone.

Be discreet. Here's a simple rule for any effective intercessor: Assume every prayer request offered by a friend is for your ears only, even if she doesn't specifically say so.

Be sensitive. While we want to demonstrate concern for

others, there's no reason to make them relive the ordeal by asking a lot of questions. All we really need to do is let them know we love them and we're praying.

Be encouraging. An encouraging card or a sympathetic promise to pray for someone in pain can brighten a dreary day and lift a weary heart. A simple expression of concern can be an incredible source of encouragement to anyone going through a physical, spiritual, or emotional struggle.

Be organized. When you make a commitment to pray for someone, make a note of it. Most people find a prayer diary extremely helpful. By keeping track of when you begin to pray and when your request is answered, you'll discover a new sense of awe at the power of prayer.

> *God is the one constant in life. And we can be
> assured he always hears our prayers.*
> SUSAN ASHTON

Be committed. If you consistently have trouble making time for prayer, find a partner and hold each other accountable. You don't necessarily have to pray together; just remind each other regularly of your commitment to pray. Share prayer requests and discuss how God has answered them. It will remind both of you of God's faithfulness and provide an opportunity to praise him together.

Whatever your individual style of intercessory prayer—group, family, or individual—remember what you're doing is important. In promising to pray for someone, you've made a sacred commitment. It's a solemn responsibility—with incredible rewards. **_Laura J. Barker_**

A Step Further

How to Start a Prayer Diary

1. *Buy a journal or notebook.*
2. *Write down a list of requests to pray for.*
3. *Break your list up into seven categories:*
   i.e., salvation, sickness, service (church
   leaders, missionaries, etc.), spiritual
   struggles, marital struggles, work
   struggles, and other.
4. *Pray separately for each category.* You
   may want to pray every Monday for the
   spiritual-struggles category, for example.
5. *Set aside a specific time to pray through*
   your prayer diary, whether it's once a
   day or once a week. Try to choose a
   time when you won't be disturbed.
6. *Record God's answers next to the requests*
   so you can see his faithfulness at work.

LJB

Faith Focus

Do you treat praying for others as a sacred responsibility, as the Old Testament prophet Samuel did (see 1 Sam. 12:23)? The Bible provides many examples of "prayer warriors," including Epaphras (see Col. 4:12) and the apostle Paul (see Rom 1:9-10; Eph. 3:14-19; 1 Thess. 1:2-3). What steps can you take today to become a prayer warrior like Samuel, Epaphras, and the apostle Paul?

Prayer Pointer

Thank God for always listening to your prayers and for interceding on behalf of those you pray for. Ask the Lord to help you make good on your good intentions to pray for others, despite busyness or interruptions.

How sweet are your words to my taste; they are sweeter than honey. Your commandments give me understanding; no wonder I hate every false way of life. Your word is a lamp for my feet and a light for my path. I've promised it once, and I'll promise again: I will obey your wonderful laws.

Psalm 119:103-106

$\mathcal{W}$alk into any Christian bookstore and you'll find aisles of books, novels, and magazines to help stimulate your faith. But when it comes to knowing what you believe and allowing the truth of God's Word to transform your daily life, there's nothing like the real thing. The Bible is the only book that can lead you to an intimate relationship with God. It contains words of truth and grace, forgiveness and healing, wisdom and strength. It's truly a "lamp for your feet and a light for your path." Making God's Word a priority can affect entire families—for the good.

Are You Rooted in the Word?

As a Graham, I'm often asked, "What's the real Billy Graham like?" I enjoy telling them that the public and private Billy Graham are no different. My brothers, sisters, and I always knew God was central in our home because he was so loved and honored by both our parents. By my father's example, I knew that God was great and Jesus was Lord. My mother, Ruth Bell Graham, was a wonderful role model, too—a woman of prayer and the Word. If I stayed up late to study for an exam and went downstairs to speak to Mother, I'd find her on her knees in prayer. Early in the morning she'd be sitting at her desk reading her Bible. And during the day, if she had a few minutes, she'd slip back to her desk again to read some more.

My mother has said, "You can't teach your children to enjoy spinach if every time they see you eating it, you gag." In the same way, you can't teach children to love and serve the Lord if they see you dreading it, complaining about it, or not doing it at all. You have to set an example. My mother had such a joyous love for the Lord and such an energy for studying the Word that I wanted a relationship with him like she had.

Because of my parents, I realized how crucial being rooted in God's Word was. Each day I need to draw strength from God through prayer and his Word in order to be the wife, mother, speaker, and writer God wants me to be.

When someone asks me, "Why is it important to study the Bible?" I respond, "Is it important for you to eat?" Bible reading and study are as basic to your Christian growth as food is to your physical health! You can take "food supplements"—other Christian books, seminars, and videos—but there's no substitute for the Word itself.

The Bible was written for ordinary people like you and me. It's thrilling to see that it's more than just history, poetry, prophecy, promises, or "thou shalt not." It's God speaking to us personally. The Bible can transform your life—and that of your family—when you begin to listen to him speak to you through his Word.

We will not understand everything in our lifetime. But as we seek God's face, study His Word, and listen to godly counsel, we understand more of God's truth. He clarifies our thinking.
MARILYN WILLETT HEAVILIN

For instance, when many of us live as if today is permanent and the only thing to live for is the present moment, the book of Revelation helps. It tells us that one day Jesus will set all the wrong right, truth will prevail over lies, and love will win over hate. Regardless of the past or present, we can be confident of a glorious future because it belongs to him!

Through my study of God's Word, I'm constantly reminded that my life on earth is just a brief blip on God's timeline. Yet living my life to please God, through service for him and a personal relationship with him, has eternal significance. *Anne Graham Lotz*

A Step Further

Focusing on the Word

1. *Have a daily quiet time.* Set aside a routine time and place for Bible reading and reflection. (Hint: Write it on your calendar!)
2. *Join a church small group or Bible study.* Groups offer consistency and encouragement to stick with Bible study.
3. *Memorize Scripture once a week.* Write a verse or passage on a 3 x 5 card and review it during the day. You'll fulfill Colossians 3:16: "Let the words of Christ, in all their richness, live in your hearts and make you wise."
4. *Skip a meal one day and let God's Word feed your soul.*
5. *Consider dropping activities that keep you from the Word.* Find a friend to hold you accountable, and do the same for her.
6. *Read a chapter in Proverbs to correspond with the day of the month.*   RCT

Faith Focus

How rooted are you in God's Word? What parts of the Bible encourage or challenge you? Which parts are you the least familiar with? How can you realistically make the Bible a more regular and intimate part of your life?

Prayer Pointer

Ask God to give you the desire and the time to seek him earnestly. Thank him for each hour he gives you, and ask him to help you be creative in finding new ways to make studying his Word a priority.

GREAT IS HIS FAITHFULNESS; HIS
MERCIES BEGIN AFRESH EACH DAY.
I SAY TO MYSELF, "THE LORD IS MY
INHERITANCE; THEREFORE, I WILL
HOPE IN HIM!" THE LORD IS WON-
DERFULLY GOOD TO THOSE WHO
WAIT FOR HIM AND SEEK HIM.

LAMENTATIONS 3:23-25

*M*y friend Cherise *hates* surprises. Last year after some girlfriends threw her a surprise birthday party, she admitted to me, "It was sweet of them, but my heart sank when I walked in the door and everyone yelled, 'Surprise!' I wish they'd have told me about it instead."

Surprises are sometimes good and sometimes bad. But God assures us, as Christians, that no matter what happens, he is "wonderfully good." He encourages us to look for his mercies each day. So don't let God's surprises pass you by. Keep an eye out for them!

Looking for God's Surprises

"Mom, are we going to Dayville for the Fourth of July?" my son, Tyler, asks, planning his summer.

"Oh yes!" I assure him. "Dayville's the only place I ever want to be on the Fourth."

Though I've never lived there, the tiny town of Dayville, Oregon, is my mother's birthplace and where I spent most summers and holidays as a child. Although it has barely two hundred residents, it glitters like a colossal sparkler on the Fourth of July.

The day kicks off with a cross-country horse race and ends with fireworks in the park. In between are barbeques, a mini rodeo, and everyone's favorite—the parade down Main Street, complete with floats, crepe-paper streamers, balloons, and tons of candy tossed out to the bystanders.

Since a parade can't very well be held amidst traffic, the townspeople simply block off the road—which also happens to be State Highway 26. When the parade ends, the roadblocks are removed, and traffic is finally allowed to drive through town. Every year we clap and cheer for each car, as if they, too, are part of the parade.

Most travelers enjoy participating in this unexpected slice of Americana. They'll give us their best beauty-pageant wave as we cheer. Some, however, irritated over the delay, pointedly ignore us.

One year, when an unusually grumpy couple drove through, my brother tossed several pieces of his collected candy into their rolled-down window, startling the couple with an unexpected treat. A few moments later, they grinned sheepishly and returned our waves. From then on, tossing candy to travelers became a family tradition.

As I look forward to another Fourth of July in Dayville, I think of the travelers whose holiday plans will take them down Highway 26—and the annual roadblock. Will they relax and enjoy the unexpected experience—or will they be so concerned with their schedule they'll miss the quaint pleasure of a small-town celebration?

> *God's surprises remind us of who's in control.*
> *He knows us better than we do, and he wants us to*
> *give our relationships—the beginnings, middles,*
> *and endings—to him.*
> ELIZABETH CODY NEWENHUYSE

Like those travelers, I often miss the surprises God tosses my way when I'm too focused on my own agenda. When my son asks me to ride bikes, will I cheat myself out of sharing his excitement over the new trail he's found because I'm too concerned about my to-do list to take the time? Or when I turn down a friend's lunch invitation because I'm too busy, will I miss being the first to hear her ecstatic announcement "I'm pregnant!"?

The Dayville parade is my annual reminder to "lighten up" and be more flexible in all areas of my life. And it's taught me to be on the lookout for God's surprises. Perhaps the woman spreading out her checkered cloth next to mine at the Fourth of July picnic will be a new friend—if I take time to introduce myself. And maybe I'm the surprise he has for her!   *Mayo Mathers*

95

A Step Further

Surprising Strategies

1. *Build "flex" time into your schedule.* Then when surprises happen, they won't throw you.
2. *Start a "Surprising Results" jar.* When a surprise occurs, good or bad, write it down on a slip of paper. Put it in the jar, and then record what happens later. You'll be amazed to see how God works everything for good (Rom. 8:28)!
3. *Spring some loving surprises on others.* Take a discouraged friend her favorite dessert, or accompany a child to a carnival. The more you do "spontaneous" things yourself, the less disturbed you'll be when your own plans are interrupted.
4. *Decide how you'll respond before a surprise— good or bad—threatens to sidetrack you.* Carrying a notecard in my wallet with writer Oswald Chambers's words "We live by God's surprises" reminds me to handle surprises with an eternal perspective.   RCT

Faith Focus

How do you handle God's surprises? Do you eagerly anticipate them, knowing they'll help you grow? Or are you like some of Dayville's travelers, annoyed because they interrupt your carefully made plans? How can you accommodate your schedule to allow time for the unexpected?

Prayer Pointer

Thank God for making you and for knowing you so well that he understands what surprises you can handle. Ask him to help you be gracious rather than grumpy, to be heavenly minded instead of earthly minded. Renew your commitment to trust everything—surprises included—to God's care.

Don't store up treasures here on earth, where they can be eaten by moths and get rusty, and where thieves break in and steal. Store your treasures in heaven, where they will never become moth-eaten or rusty and where they will be safe from thieves. Wherever your treasure is, there your heart and thoughts will also be.

Matthew 6:19-21

*Y*our new car. The piano your grandfather gave you. A favorite chair. Your computer. A diamond necklace. Your just-built deck. Your remodeled kitchen. Your collection of music boxes. A new winter wardrobe.

Material things. Who isn't tempted to have more, to buy more? When others seem to have more than we do, it's tempting to "keep up with the Joneses." After all, we deserve it, don't we? But Scripture asks us to think long-range, rather than short-term, about where our treasure truly should reside. Here's how a seeming tragedy helped one woman discover her heart's true home.

There's No Place like Home

It was the first day back to preschool after Christmas break, and my three sons and I were off to a slow start. It was four degrees below zero outside, so I was in no hurry to take them to afternoon preschool. Still dressed in our pajamas, we sat munching on peanut butter sandwiches for lunch.

As we ate in the kitchen on the main floor, flames from an old stove licked at the walls and scorched the ceiling below us in the family room. Oblivious to the danger we were in (the smoke detectors malfunctioned and never sounded), I sent my three children to their basement bedroom to get dressed for the day. When I went to check on their progress five minutes later, smoke streamed through the downstairs hall into their bedroom where they played with their toys, unaware of what was happening. Panic-stricken, I dashed from room to room, yelling, "What's burning?"

When I got to the end of the hall, our family room was engulfed in flames. "Run!" I shouted. We tore out of the basement door and ran down the block in bare feet, frantically knocking on neighbors' doors for help.

In the safety of my friend's living room across the street, I held my boys tightly, comforting them and thanking God we were safe. Waves of shock rode through me as I realized I'd lost everything. Where will we go now that our home has been destroyed? I wept. How can we cope without our things? What will we do without picture memories of our children?

But through that experience, gradually it dawned on me that everything I have is because of God's grace—whether it's my next breath or our next paycheck. Slowly—painfully—I began to recognize the difference between what is mine (nothing) and what is God's (everything). Like iron that's purified in the white heat of a furnace, God used the fire to reveal my tendency to find more security in the things of this world than in his promises to care for us.

After the contractors completely gutted and rebuilt the interior of the duplex, we moved back in and began reestablishing our home. Starting from scratch, I've been able to add back into our lives things that enhance it rather than clutter our living space. For instance, we allow each of our kids three shelves on which to store their toys. When this space is full, they can't add anything more until they've given up something they no longer use. Similarly, I keep in my closet only clothes and shoes I wear regularly.

> *Who isn't tempted by material things? But when I am, I ask myself, "What's more important—my relationship with God or these temporary things?" That always gives me perspective.*
> CeCe Winans

Paring down our lifestyle has freed up more time to spend with each other instead of maintaining our possessions like I used to do. That's not to say we're never challenged by the lure of accumulating more. But one thing I do know for certain: To lose was to gain. Outwardly, we have less. But what remains on the interior—the contents of my heart—is the security of knowing I have an indestructible home with God. *Marian V. Liautaud*

A STEP FURTHER

Putting Stuff in Perspective

1. *Go through your closets.* If you haven't worn an item of clothing or used that sports equipment within the last year, give it away to a charitable cause.

2. *Look through sale flyers only when you need a particular item.* Otherwise, seeing items on sale only makes you *think* you need them.

3. *Remember that just because something's a good deal doesn't mean it's for you.* That home may look perfect, but will it strap you financially? That new coat may be on sale, but if you don't need a new coat, you're wasting your money.

4. *Befriend those who have less than you.* You can use your "wealth" to help someone else, plus you won't have to worry about keeping up with the Joneses! RCT

Faith Focus

When are you most tempted to want more or to spend too much? Do you have any possessions that might possess you? If so, which ones? Since God calls us to share what we have with others—whether it's an extra bedroom, a car, or a gift for baking or baby-sitting—what could you share this week?

Prayer Pointer

Praise God for all the wonderful blessings he's granted you—a place to live, transportation, friends, family, etc. Invite him to show you what "things" you cling to—and give them back to him. Then ask him to help you use your "wealth" in these areas to make an eternal difference for Christ and his kingdom.

When you go through deep waters and great trouble, I will be with you. When you go through rivers of difficulty, you will not drown! When you walk through the fire of oppression, you will not be burned up; the flames will not consume you. For I am the Lord, your God, the Holy One of Israel, your Savior.

Isaiah 43:2-3

*H*ave you ever wondered what God's up to? Why the guy you thought was so perfect for you walked out of your life? Why your work seems so difficult and unfulfilling? Why the friends you trusted betrayed your confidence and gossiped to other members of your church? Why you had to move—in the dead of winter? Why your child chose not to follow Christ, even after all those years in church?

Why do we always ask *why*? Because we're human and incessantly curious. But here's why we don't always get an answer to our questions—and what we can hold on to in the meantime.

Why Ask Why?

My mom married at age twenty-one, and I fully expected to be married with children by the time I was in my mid-twenties. A few broken engagements later, I'm now in my mid-thirties and still single, with no obvious prospects for a spouse. On many a night, I crawl into bed pondering Ecclesiastes 4:11 ("How can one be warm alone?") and find myself asking, "Why, God? Why am I single? Why can't I have a husband and children?"

The *why* question is a popular prayer because life often seems so unfair. We wonder why good things happen to bad people—and bad things to good people. Why does the uncomplaining, middle-aged pastor's wife have to endure years of cancer, painfully slow recoveries, and the threat of no more insurance? Why do Christians get persecuted? And why does God allow tragedies like floods, earthquakes, and terrorist attacks?

The truth is, outside of the fact that we live in a sin-cursed world, we may never know why certain things happen. We do know that God is holy, righteous, all-powerful, and in control. He decrees everything according to his infinite wisdom and sovereign will. Even Jesus' agonizing crucifixion on the cross was no accident. Christ endured the dreadful curse to save our souls, so he can certainly understand our trials and difficulties—and give us the strength and power to endure them. We may want our pain or suffering to cease, for example, but Christ might reply, "My grace is sufficient for you, for my power is made perfect in weakness" (2 Cor. 12:9, NIV).

At times the truth of this Scripture may be hard to

accept. Some people would rather believe that suffering is not the Christian's domain, that it indicates a lack of faith. But Joni Eareckson Tada, a quadriplegic, has pointed out that it takes a lot of faith to smile though confined to a wheelchair for more than thirty years. In fact, faith is the key in choosing to leave the *whys* of life up to God.

> *Surrendering our will to God's will, choosing to trust God, allows us to begin making faith-filled decisions.*
>
> CAROL KENT

Even if we don't know why troubles come, God can use them for a good greater than we can ever imagine. Think of the untold thousands who have been helped through Joni's testimony. We aren't here for our own pleasure or comfort; we're here to glorify Christ and model his love, patience, and perseverance to others as we look forward to our Savior's return.

So what about my singleness? What if God doesn't answer my prayer for a mate and children of my own? I guess I'll just save up for a down comforter for my bed, pour myself even more into the lives of other children, and live by the truth in Psalm 27:13-14: "I am confident that I will see the Lord's goodness. . . . Be brave and courageous. Yes, wait patiently for the Lord."

Linda Piepenbrink

A Step Further

A Cure for the *Whys*

1. *Ask what instead of why.* In any circumstance you can ask yourself, What, O Lord, do you want me to do with this situation for your glory?
2. *Read Scripture passages where others are asking why.* In particular, look at the book of Job and the Psalms where the writers asked a lot of *why* questions and were answered in some surprising ways. Reading what God says in his Word will help to put our *whys* in perspective.
3. *Get on with the business of living.* Don't get mired in the past. Some *whys* won't be answered until we can ask God in heaven, so there's no use spending our precious earthly time continually asking *why*.

RCT

Faith Focus

At what times in your life have you asked *why* (maybe it was during a difficult birth of a child or when a speeding motorist slammed into your just-paid-off vehicle)? What have you learned about yourself and God as a result of these experiences? If you're currently in the middle of a difficult time, how will you choose to respond—with a complaining spirit or with patient faith, praising God for his work in your life?

Prayer Pointer

Praise God that he knows everything—even the answer to all your *whys*. Thank him for his wisdom in sometimes revealing, sometimes concealing the answers to your questions. Pray that you'll accept circumstances even when you don't understand, and continue to praise him in the process.

Do not worship any other gods besides me. Do not make idols of any kind.... You must never worship or bow down to them, for I, the Lord your God, am a jealous God who will not share your affection with any other God! ... But I lavish my love on those who love me and obey my commands, even for a thousand generations.

Exodus 20:3-6

*W*hat's important to you? Your state-of-the-art computer? A new dress for your upcoming banquet? Having the best manicured lawn on the street?

Examining what's important to us is a good way of discovering what we consider as a high priority. With the world's emphasis on materialism, it's so easy to fall into the traps of "getting ahead" and "looking good." But God makes it clear in his Word: "Do not worship any other gods besides me" (Exod. 20:3).

What does he mean by "other gods"? The answer is often much closer to our everyday life than we think.

Everyday Idols

Years ago, I took my four-year-old son to the local pet store. As he meandered through the rows of aquariums, I stopped to look at terra-cotta statues of dogs and cats. But when my son rounded the corner and caught sight of the statues, he gasped and ran to me in wide-eyed earnestness, exclaiming, "Mommy! Lookit those idols! We better get outta here!" Obviously, he'd taken the golden calf stories in Sunday school to heart and didn't want to risk getting mixed up with idol worshipers!

For many of us, the mention of idols brings up visions of multi-armed goddesses enthroned in eastern temples. It's easy for us to look back at the Israelites and their fall into idol worship with a mixture of disdain and incredulity. How can people be so gullible? we ask ourselves. How could they bow before golden calves when God had pushed walls of water aside for them, showered them with daily food, led them with a cloud by day and fire by night? What were they thinking?

But today we, too, stray into idol worship when something—anything—other than God becomes the focus of our hearts. The apostle Paul warns us against this covetousness in Ephesians 5:5. When we worship "the things of this world," we end up with a bad case of the "divided heart syndrome." King David was a prime example of this malady as he toyed with lust, dabbled in power, and manipulated truth for his purposes.

But I'm guilty of the same thing every time I spend an afternoon at the mall blindly admiring sleekly dressed mannequins. The seed of dissatisfaction is sown in my heart, and suddenly my clothes are dumpy, my hair outdated, and my house frowzy. In short, the eternal things of God are relegated to a distant place—after a classy winter coat, a chic haircut, or a new couch.

How can any of us flee from these subtle (and not so subtle) kinds of idolatry? How can we recognize them for what they are and shout, "Lookit those idols! We better get outta here!"?

God wishes to instill within each of us a strong desire for the imperishable, for the incorruptible, for the inheritance that never perishes, spoils, or fades.
JONI EARECKSON TADA

If we don't know what God is really like, if we have not worshiped in his presence, if we have not filled ourselves with his Word, then how can we possibly recognize God's presence in our lives? We need to ask God to give us an undivided heart—a heart of love for him that won't allow anything other than God to become the ultimate concern of our life.

As we seek to love God and live our lives for Christ, we must be willing to recognize, confess, and deal with our own idols of the heart. The writer of I John exhorts us with more tenderness than my son's warning, but his message is no less fervent or contemporary: "Dear children, keep yourselves from idols" (I John 5:21, NIV).

Lauretta Patterson

A Step Further

Safeguards against Idols

1. *Pray to stay devoted.* Asking God to fill us with love for him is the place to start (Ps. 86:1).
2. *Recognize the real thing.* The more time you spend in God's Word, the better you'll be able to discern what is false.
3. *Don't substitute the good for the best.* Remember that even good, worthwhile things—like spending time with family and friends—can become a substitute for God.
4. *Examine your own heart.* Knowing your own heart—that center of all drives, emotions, and moral choices—will help you guard against potential idols.
5. *Confess any wrong desires.* Then take steps to put your life in the right perspective, with God as first priority.   LP

Faith Focus

What "things" do you treat as first priority in your life? Are any "gods" lurking around the corner and side-tracking you from loving what's eternal—God and his Word?

In what ways do your actions show that you love the Lord *first*, above all else (see Matt. 22:36-37)?

Prayer Pointer

Thank God for the Life Manual he's given you to help you determine his priorities. Ask him to point out any "gods" that may be sidetracking your faith. Then commit yourself to make firm plans to put—and keep—your priorities in line with his will.

[JOB SAID,] "IF ONLY I KNEW WHERE TO FIND GOD, I WOULD GO TO HIS THRONE AND TALK WITH HIM THERE. . . . I GO EAST, BUT HE IS NOT THERE. I GO WEST, BUT I CANNOT FIND HIM. I DO NOT SEE HIM IN THE NORTH, FOR HE IS HIDDEN. I TURN TO THE SOUTH, BUT I CANNOT FIND HIM. BUT HE KNOWS WHERE I AM GOING. . . . FOR I HAVE STAYED IN GOD'S PATHS; I HAVE FOLLOWED HIS WAYS AND NOT TURNED ASIDE."

JOB 23:3, 8-11

$\mathcal{H}$ ave you ever felt as if you've lost God's phone number? You're dialing constantly, but you can't seem to get through? Either the line's busy, or he's not picking up. Or maybe the line is even disconnected.

All of us face times when God seems silent. We wonder if we've failed in some way and caused God to remove his presence from us, or if God simply isn't there. Spiritual dryness can shake our faith to the core.

But if we see spiritual blahs as normal, they don't have to be threatening to our faith. They can actually be a blessing in disguise!

Feeling Spiritually Blah?

I was twenty-one when I hit my first spiritual dry spell. I had accepted Christ as a child and took my faith seriously through my teen years. I had established a habit of regular quiet times and had set my sights on a life of Christian service. I knew what it was to feel close to the Lord, and I enjoyed fellowship with him in the Word and prayer.

During my senior year in college, however, I contracted a bad case of spiritual blahs. God felt far away. Reading the Bible was flat, and praying seemed like a fruitless ritual. I experienced a sense of discomfort that sucked the joy out of my life.

I tried all the remedies I knew. I looked for sins to confess. I repented of everything I thought might be wrong in my life. I read Scripture, hoping for some injection of truth. I prayed, but God seemed distant.

Some months later I wondered if my sense of soul-dryness wasn't a symptom of exhaustion; I was a new bride who worked fifteen hours a week while finishing my last year of college.

One Sunday afternoon it dawned on me that if sin was the reason I felt so dry, then it was the Holy Spirit's job to let me know that. After all, Jesus had called the Spirit my Convictor. I could count on him to show me if I were truly out of fellowship with God.

This insight prompted me to pray, "Father, you know I love you, and I know you will convict me when sin gets in the way of our relationship. So I'm going to believe that the connection between us is unbroken unless the Spirit lets me know otherwise." Committing myself to him in this way enabled me to remove the focus from feelings of dryness to rejoicing in the reality of my bond with him—a bond he has pledged to nurture.

A couple of years later, I again felt spiritually low. At the time I was wrestling with the fact that the doors to ministry seemed to slam in my face. The thought crossed my mind, *Maybe God doesn't consider me usable in his kingdom.*

> *God doesn't promise life is going to be easy.*
> *He just promises to be there for us.*
> BODIE THOENE

Since misery loves company, I opened my Bible to the book of Job. I expected to have a good pity party along with another who wondered where God was. Then I came across these words of Job: "I cannot find him. But he knows where I am going" (Job 23:9-10).

Light penetrated the darkness with the understanding that God knows the way I take. I am not hidden to him; he continually watches over me. So what if I don't feel he's close to me? The fact remains: He's there for me whether I sense his presence or not. And that truth can shake any spiritual blahs.   ***Pamela Hoover Heim***

A Step Further

Watering a Dry Spell?

1. *Realize that feelings are fickle.* You won't always experience emotional highs in your relationship with God.
2. *Rely on God's promises.* God's Word says he loves us and never leaves us. That means we can relish the times when we sense his closeness, but we don't have to go into a tailspin when we have to walk by faith in his promises.
3. *Remember, being dry can be good.* Feeling lonely for God prompts us toward intimacy with him. When the disciple Thomas demanded that Jesus prove his resurrection, our Savior said, "You believe because you have seen me. Blessed are those who haven't seen me and believe anyway" (John 20:29). Dry times force us to live not by sight but by faith. PHH

Faith Focus

When have you felt spiritually blah? Was it because of a critical life event (e.g., the death of a spouse or parent, the transition from working outside the home to becoming a stay-at-home mom, a breakup with a potential spouse)? Have the blahs come during times of physical fatigue? Have they been the result of your own apathy toward God or resentment toward life circumstances?

How can remembering God's promise to never leave you be an antidote to your spiritual doldrums?

Prayer Pointer

Make these words from the psalmist your prayer: "Lord, give to me your unfailing love. . . . I honor and love your commands. I meditate on your principles. Remember your promise to me, for it is my only hope. Your promise revives me; it comforts me in all my troubles" (Ps. 119:41, 48-50).

BE TRULY GLAD! THERE IS WON-
DERFUL JOY AHEAD, EVEN
THOUGH IT IS NECESSARY FOR YOU
TO ENDURE MANY TRIALS FOR A
WHILE. THESE TRIALS ARE ONLY
TO TEST YOUR FAITH, TO SHOW
THAT IT IS STRONG AND PURE. IT
IS BEING TESTED AS FIRE TESTS
AND PURIFIES GOLD—AND YOUR
FAITH IS FAR MORE PRECIOUS TO
GOD THAN MERE GOLD.

1 PETER 1:6-7

DAY 21

 $\mathcal{T}$ he night my friend Cassie gave birth to her second child, we gathered around her hospital room and prayed. Cassie's baby had died in her womb because the cord had wrapped around his neck.

Yet Cassie's faith remained strong. A week later, she told me tearfully, "This is awful, but God's still faithful. And if it helps me identify with other women who lose their babies, it'll be worth it." Today Cassie and her husband are missionaries in a country where few children live to see their fifth birthday.

In the fire, Cassie tested gold, and we can too.

What Good Is Suffering?

Ten years ago, I had a "routine" dental procedure and was left with a severely damaged nerve in my jaw. As a result, shooting pain pulsated constantly on the right side of my face.

To rid myself of the excruciating pain, I traveled from one doctor to another for six months—to no avail. Finally, a doctor at Mayo Clinic told me, "Mrs. Mittelstaedt, there's nothing more we can do to repair the damage or relieve your pain. You'll have to live with it."

When I returned home to Germany with this news, I felt discouraged and deeply depressed. Medical records show that many people who suffer with the same problem resort to suicide. I, too, felt death was the only escape, but as a Christian, I couldn't believe that was God's will.

But the constant pain took its toll. I felt hopeless, with nothing left to hang on to. One day, during my morning walk, I crossed a small bridge near Frankfurt, looked down at the flowing river below, and was tempted to jump.

At that moment, Matthew 4:5-7 came to my mind. I recalled how the devil had unsuccessfully tempted Jesus to jump from the highest point of the temple. So I said, "No, I am not going to jump. I am going to trust God."

I began telling God what I was most afraid of—living in pain. Then I remembered that Jesus says we shouldn't worry about tomorrow—that he gives us strength for each day.

As I looked out over our town and saw its beautiful fairy-tale homes with flower boxes, white picket fences, and clean-swept sidewalks, I realized that behind this perfect facade were thousands of Europeans struggling with broken marriages, depression, guilt, and loneliness. I felt God speak to my heart, *Elizabeth, these women are suffering like you are today, but their pain is different—it's emotional.*

I no longer felt so alone in my pain. And suddenly I was filled with a desire to encourage those women. That morning, the vision for a Christian woman's magazine in Europe was born.

> *When you cling to the truth of God's love,*
> *you can find blessing even in pain.*
> TRACEY D. BUCHANAN

Almost a decade has passed since that day by the bridge. Today, *Lydia* is printed in three languages and reaches about one million readers. Its message is simple— hope and encouragement can be found through faith in Christ and his Word. Pain is still my companion—but it's no longer as overwhelming as it once was. When I searched God's Word for encouragement and comfort, I came upon Psalm 34:19: "The righteous face many troubles, but the Lord rescues them from each and every one." The words to the left of the comma describe my circumstances, and the words to the right give me hope. But I've learned that when we hang on to the comma in the middle—wait in faith on God's promise and offer our pain to him—it's never wasted.   *Elizabeth Mittelstaedt*

A Step Further

Softening the Sorrow

1. *Accept suffering as allowed by God.* However, this doesn't mean it's wrong to battle a disease with medicines or to confront and correct injustice.
2. *Allow others to minister to you.* Ask for prayer, companionship, and accept help.
3. *Simplify your life so you have time to pray and reflect.* Don't overload your calendar with appointments or long to-do lists.
4. *Turn to the Scriptures.* Since God creates each person uniquely, there's no one right answer for all situations. But the Bible presents a wide range of insights as to the *why* and the benefits of suffering.
5. *Read books by fellow sufferers.* You might not feel so alone in your situation.
6. *Be creative.* Those who suffer often are motivated to help others by launching a ministry of some kind.   RCT

Faith Focus

When have you suffered—whether little or much? Was it when you discovered a friend had cancer? or that you were infertile? Or was it when you went through a period of discouragement? Did that situation bring you closer to God or push you further from him? The next time you face suffering, will you choose to become bitter or call on God's help and comfort?

Prayer Pointer

Praise God for his almighty power to help you through troubling times. Tell him you will trust him—no matter what happens in your life. Ask him to show you ways in which your past and present sufferings can teach the watching world that he's trustworthy.

Don't copy the behavior and customs of this world, but let God transform you into a new person by changing the way you think. Then you will know what God wants you to do, and you will know how good and pleasing and perfect his will really is.

Romans 12:2

It was just a little white lie. What's the big deal?"

- "We're not gossiping. We're praying for him."
- "Who will know if I do that? It won't hurt anybody."
- "If I told her the truth, she'd get mad."
- "That guy's ripped me off so many times. I'm certainly not going to tell him he undercharged me for his hours."

We've all heard these justifications for minor sins; maybe we've even used them ourselves. But are "minor" sins really so minor after all? Should we take more caution?

The Major Problem with "Minor Sins"

A few weeks ago, I pulled into my driveway after stopping at the local gas station for a fill-up. I lowered myself out of the van on the lift, pushed the button to close the door, then noticed my gas cap was missing. The attendant had forgotten to put it back on. *Oh brother!* I fumed. Exasperated because it's tougher to get around as a physically disabled person, I opened the door, lowered the lift, wheeled into the van, and drove back to the station.

I arrived at the station, got out of my van—again—and powered my chair up to the cashier's window to inquire about my gas cap. The attendant glanced around his desk. "Is this yours?" he asked as he held up a stainless steel gas cap.

I hardly looked at it. Not thinking twice, I mumbled, "Yeah, that's it." As I watched him screw the cap on my van, I took a closer look. It wasn't mine.

I felt guilty. But not guilty enough to keep me from driving around for a few days with the hot gas cap. Hummph! They were the ones who lost it in the first place . . . why shouldn't I take one of theirs?

A few nights later, however, I stumbled across Hebrews 3:13 in my quiet time: "You must warn each other every day . . . so that none of you will be deceived by sin and hardened against God." No sooner had I closed my Bible than the gas-cap scene replayed in my mind.

The next morning I bought a new gas cap at an auto supply store, pulled into the gas station again, and flagged the attendant over. "I did a very wrong thing when I took that cap last week. I lied. It wasn't mine and I am very sorry.

Here," I said, motioning toward the box on my dashboard, "take this new one in return."

"You went out and got a new cap?" He scratched his head, bewildered. "No, forget about it; it's nothing. We have a bunch of them."

I wish he'd realized the whole exercise was more for my sake than his. Sure, I know God will forgive me if I repent of my lies, but I'm also aware that making excuses for any sin will harden me—it will make my heart calloused and insensitive to evil. Now I have Hebrews 3:13 and a sun-faded, never-opened boxed gas cap on my dash to remind me just how deceitful sin really is.

> *If I am willing to do an honest after-the-fact evaluation of my wrong and sinful choices, God can use my understanding to guarantee his outcome in my life.*
>
> MARLENE D. LeFEVER

Why sweat the small stuff? I've been through enough of those minor "gas cap" skirmishes against sin to know that our struggle to be holy is a major battle. No matter how major or minor sin seems, we cannot alter its offensive nature and repulsive character in the sight of God.

But God is honestly delighted and excited when I obey. I can just picture the Spirit cheering me on as I drove into that gas station prepared with an apology and a reparation. Now *that's* what makes me strive to be holy.

Joni Eareckson Tada

A STEP FURTHER

Striving for Holiness

1. *Obey the nudgings of the Spirit—immediately.* Then you won't have to feel guilty or say "I'm sorry" so often!
2. *Repent.* You always have to ask God for forgiveness when you sin, and you may need to ask another person, too.
3. *Decide you won't do it again.* Make plans to not get yourself into that situation again.
4. *Ask someone you trust to pray regularly with and for you.* You don't have to do this in person—it can be over the phone. But have someone hold you accountable to a transformed life.
5. *Keep a reminder of a past failure.* Just as the gas cap was Joni's reminder to always strive to be holy, what could you use?

RCT

Faith Focus

Are there any "minor" sins lurking in the corners of your life? If so, what are they? How can you use verses such as Ephesians 6:13-18 to stand firm against temptations? The next time you're tempted with a "minor" sin, what will you say or do?

Prayer Pointer

Thank God for his work in perfecting you for his glory. Ask him to help you resist even those falsehoods that seem so "minor." Pray that you'll always be found "standing firm," so you'll continue to be a light of his truth to the world.

See how very much our heavenly Father loves us, for he allows us to be called his children, and we really are! . . . Yes, dear friends, we are already God's children, and we can't even imagine what we will be like when Christ returns. But we do know that when he comes we will be like him, for we will see him as he really is.

1 John 3:1-2

*M*aybe your dad lectured you continually, always worked late, or didn't live with you at all because he divorced your mom.

Fathers—we're all affected by memories of times spent with or without them. Since psychologists say a child's view of the world and God is often "most informed by their father," it's no wonder some of us struggle with thinking of God as our heavenly Father.

But unlike human fathers, God is perfect. As we unravel some common "lies" about who he is and discover the truth, we can learn how to relax as children in our perfect Dad's arms.

Is God Truly *Your Father?*

It's not unusual for a little girl to worship her daddy. I sure did. But as we mature, most of us realize our fathers weren't perfect—sometimes they made mistakes that affect how we view God as our father.

I made this discovery only recently when I came across a costume I'd worn in high school. Although my parents were separated, my dad had promised to be there the night I performed. But he never showed. I was crushed.

One costume. One memory. That's all it took to open my eyes. I'd been carrying around a lot of hurt for sixteen years. Had this experience, and others like it, tainted my concept of my heavenly Father as well?

The answer was yes. Deep down I felt I couldn't depend on God because I couldn't depend on my father. But as I began to sort the truth about who God is from the lies I was telling myself, here's what I learned.

God is not a demanding tyrant; he's a forgiving father. If you're afraid to confess your shortcomings to God for fear he'll condemn you or, worse yet, withhold his love from you, you need to know this truth: No matter how many times we fail, God loves us unconditionally. He never treats us as our sins deserve but patiently and wisely allows us to learn from our mistakes. And when we repent, he readily forgives us.

God is always there for you; he's attentive and accessible. Maybe your dad was absent or rarely home—or when he was home, he never had time to talk. But because we are God's "treasured possessions," he invites us to come to him for counsel and support *anytime*. And when we do, he responds (James 1:5).

God is dependable; he's trustworthy. For some of us, identifying God as father raises a painful question: Can I really trust God? Others of us are afraid that when we give God free rein, he'll "zap" us with some tragedy. In truth, our heavenly Father promises to treat us with love and compassion. Unlike human fathers, he'll never break a commitment, lie to us, or try to impress or manipulate us. He simply loves us (John 3:16).

> *Our view of God is always filtered through our experiences and relationships—and affects not only what we think God feels about us, but what we feel about ourselves.*
>
> KELSEY MENEHAN

God doesn't ask for performance or perfection; instead, he wants our heart. As a child, I went to great lengths to win my dad's praise. Later, I didn't feel acceptable to God unless I was working. But while we were still sinners—hardly pleasing to God—Jesus died for us. He paid an enormous price to show us what the Father is really like and to make intimacy with him possible (2 Cor. 6:18; John 14:21).

Today, as I get to know my heavenly Father for who he really is, my relationship with God is beginning to feel different. When I'm on my knees, I feel as if I'm in God's lap. And somehow, crying "Abba, Father" feels right, because finally, it's coming from my heart and not my head.

Michele Halseide

A STEP FURTHER

Looking for Love
in All the Right Places

1. *Dig into the Scriptures.* Get to know who
   God really is so you don't believe the lies
   others tell you or the lies you tell yourself.
2. *Find passages that speak to you personally
   about the fatherhood of God and your
   privileges as his daughter.*
3. *Write some of these verses on notecards.*
   Carry them with you; repeat them aloud
   every time you catch yourself slipping
   into old thought patterns.
4. *Allow God to turn your head knowledge
   about him into heart knowledge* (see Rom.
   8:15-16).
5. *Don't expect changes overnight.* If you
   struggle with God as Father, you've
   probably had years' worth of reasons. God
   is patient, and he never gives up on us.

MH

Faith Focus

Did any of your "father" relationships—with a birth father, stepfather, or adoptive father—cause you to believe lies about God such as:

- he's a demanding tyrant, instead of a forgiving father?
- he'll walk out on you, when the truth is, he's always attentive and accessible?
- you can't trust him, when God is always dependable?
- he expects you to be perfect, rather than just wanting your heart?

How can you actively reverse those lies with God's truth?

Prayer Pointer

Thank God that he's a forgiving, attentive, accessible, dependable, loving, and perfect Father! Ask him to help you see yourself as his child, with all the rewards of being his heir—he will always love you and listen eagerly to you.

Don't worry about anything; instead, pray about everything. Tell God what you need, and thank him for all he has done. If you do this, you will experience God's peace, which is far more wonderful than the human mind can understand. His peace will guard your hearts and minds as you live in Christ Jesus.

PHILIPPIANS 4:6-7

*D*o you worry about your family's safety? your overwhelming workload? what others will think if you start that ministry? your eternal security—if you're really a Christian after all?

When we can't see the big picture, as God can, sometimes we feel as though we're groping around blindly in the dark, hoping we don't run into anything. But that's not the way God calls us to live. If any doubts, worries, or fears are stripping your confidence and keeping you up at night, take heart. Here are a few ideas that will quiet those worries and help you get some sleep.

Are Your Worries Keeping
You Up at Night?

If worry ever becomes an Olympic event, I've got a chance at the gold medal. I wish I could say my worrying ended when I became a Christian, but there are still nights when I stay awake and worry about my health or deadlines or how I'm going to put my kids through college.

We all have worries—we're anxious about what the future holds. We don't know if our child will come to Christ, if our spouse will outlive us, or if that medical test will show anything suspicious. Yet when our life worries multiply out of control, here's what we need to remember: *If we've accepted God's sacrifice of his Son on our own behalf, we're his children—and he's in control.*

After my wife, Leslie, prayed to receive Christ in 1979, she didn't feel as though anything had happened. There were no fireworks, no immediate changes in her life. So Leslie would lie awake at night and worry, *If I were to die tonight, would I go to heaven?* Because of her uncertainty, she kept praying to receive Christ—just to make sure—until a mature Christian friend told her that God's Word says that, no matter your feelings from day to day, believing plus receiving equals salvation (John 1:12). If you don't have confidence about where you stand with God, review the facts (1 John 5:13), and don't base your faith on feelings.

But it's also possible that the reason you don't feel as though you are a Christian is because you're not. It wasn't until the death of my father some years ago, when I was still an atheist, that I started to face my own mortality. After his funeral, I stared into the night and wondered, *Is it really true that when we die, that's it?* Thoughts such as this one gnawed at me relentlessly.

If you're living your life without God—or you're not sure where you stand with him—ask yourself these questions: Am I living a hand-me-down faith from my parents? Do I equate church attendance with being a Christian?

Now's the time to settle the issue once and for all by accepting Christ's death on the cross as full payment for your sins and yielding your life to him.

> *I tend to be a perfectionist, and God's forgiveness released me from trying to earn my way into heaven by being "good."*
> BETSY KING

As a Christian, now I have hope. But my hope isn't based on wishful thinking or blind optimism. When the Bible talks about hope, it's inextricably linked with the historical fact of the resurrection of Jesus Christ. Scripture says we can have the hope and confidence of eternal life because Jesus Christ overcame death. Jesus says, "I am the resurrection and the life. Those who believe in me, even though they die like everyone else, will live again. They are given eternal life for believing in me and will never perish" (John 11:25-26).

That truth changes everything for me. You see, I've lived as an atheist, and I've lived as a Christian. And I've found there's no other light than that of Jesus Christ (John 8:12) to chase away the shadows that keep us tossing and turning at night.
Lee Strobel

A Step Further

Worry Busters

1. *Present your requests to God.* Tell God, "I'm anxious. This is what I'm facing and what I'm feeling."
2. *Thank him for all his promises to care for you.* Be assured that God knows all about your situation and wants the best for you.
3. *Review ways God has come through for you in the past.* (You may even want to start a journal and record requests and answers to prayer.) Thank him for the times he's come to your rescue!
4. *Make the kingdom of God your primary concern.* If you live for him, he will give you all you need to live from day to day (Matt. 6:33-34). LS

Faith Focus

What things do *you* tend to worry about? Is there anything you can do about those things? If so, why not take action (e.g., begin setting aside money for retirement)? If not, why not trust God enough to hand over your worries—and not take them back?

Prayer Pointer

Praise God for his great and mighty power over every event in the universe. Thank him for listening to and handling all the things that worry you. Ask him to help you learn to turn your "worry list" over to him *before* it makes you too anxious.

DON'T YOU KNOW THAT THE
LORD IS THE EVERLASTING GOD,
THE CREATOR OF ALL THE EARTH?
HE NEVER GROWS FAINT OR
WEARY. . . . HE GIVES POWER TO
THOSE WHO ARE TIRED AND WORN
OUT; HE OFFERS STRENGTH TO
THE WEAK. . . . THOSE WHO WAIT
ON THE LORD WILL FIND NEW
STRENGTH. THEY WILL FLY HIGH
ON WINGS LIKE EAGLES. THEY
WILL RUN AND NOT GROW WEARY.
THEY WILL WALK AND NOT FAINT.

ISAIAH 40:28-31

DAY 25

*H*ave you ever felt so overwhelmed by work, family, and church activities that you don't even have time to read the Bible for yourself? Do you struggle with getting up for your quiet time when that alarm clock goes off? Do you wonder if God has anything else better in mind for you than your current life?

All of us have thoughts like these at one time or another. (That's why I thank the Lord for Isaiah's encouraging words!) But before you begin to feel guilty and discouraged and label yourself a spiritual failure, consider what author Lauretta Patterson has to say.

147

I Don't Feel like a Very Good Christian

I met some friends for lunch the other day and after coffee, our conversation took a more serious turn.

"I feel like a terrible Christian," Debbie moaned in exasperation. "I've been crabby with the kids and stressed out at work. I haven't had a quiet time in days—and for the past three weeks, I've just thrown my Sunday school lesson together. This sure doesn't feel like the 'abundant life' we Christians are supposed to have!"

If you long for a fruitful life that reflects the Lord's character but often feel overcommitted, underdisciplined, and anything but Spirit-filled, how can you move beyond feeling like a failure as a Christian to resting in your status as a beloved child of God?

Sometimes the most straightforward explanation is that we're tired and need rest! How many of us women wake up early to squeeze in a quiet time, run around all day accomplishing several tasks, then dash to an evening activity? No wonder we drag in our spiritual lives! God made us physical beings with hormonal cycles, body rhythms, and the need for rest. Giving yourself a restful day once a week may be just the spiritual boost you need to help you rest in the truth of God's Word and who you are in his eyes instead of rehashing what you can and can't do.

It also helps to have a community—other Christians you can talk with and pray with. Not only can Christian fellowship draw us into effective ministry, it also can take us out of places we don't belong. Those of us who are nurturers by nature can easily commit to people, programs, or issues that may or may not be God's focus for our attention at that time.

We desperately need the perspective and prayers of fellow Christians to sort out what our true priorities should be.

It's so easy for us to fall into the "activism" mentality of our culture—by collecting extensive lists of involvements and achievements to validate our worth. Unfortunately, this mentality can carry over into our spiritual life. We may measure our spirituality by our answers to questions such as: How regular is my quiet time? What Christian books am I reading? How active am I in my church? How much time am I spending with the needy?

The irony of our spiritual life is that the sheer volume of Christian activities may squeeze out our relationship with the Lord. We end up feeling like terrible Christians even while accomplishing things that seem worthwhile.

As Christians, we should accept failure as a part of growth. We have the wonderful freedom to fail, and still be loved.

MARGARET BECKER

Ultimately, it's the Spirit's work in our life that makes us grow spiritually. It's not something we can "work up" ourselves—and it's not going to look the same for everyone.

The mystery of Emmanuel, God with us, is that he already is with us—and we don't have to jump through any behavior hoop in order to snuggle in his arms. Even when we feel like failures as Christians, our Shepherd lifts us close to him with tenderness and compassion—until we're ready to walk alongside in perfect confidence. *Lauretta Patterson*

A STEP FURTHER

Rejuvenate Your Spiritual Life!

1. *When you're tired, take a time-out.* Enjoy rather than strive; relax rather than achieve.
2. *Don't listen to Satan's discouragement.* Don't fall for the "I'm a failure" trap.
3. *Go out of your way to develop Christian friends*—whether in your neighborhood, at church, your night class, your child's play group, etc.
4. *Don't fall for the "activism" mentality of today's culture.* Live life with joy and purpose, instead of just rushing around.
5. *Remember that God walks beside you.* He's listening, and he's ready to help you—anytime.   LP

Faith Focus

What things strip spiritual joy from you and make you feel like a failure as a Christian? How can Bible promises such as the following help you?

- "We can be mirrors that brightly reflect the glory of the Lord. And as the Spirit of the Lord works within us, we become more and more like him and reflect his glory even more" (2 Cor. 3:18).
- "I am sure that God, who began the good work within you, will continue his work until it is finally finished on that day when Christ Jesus comes back again" (Phil. 1:6).

Prayer Pointer

Thank God that he truly is our "strength" and someone to be trusted (see Isa. 30:15). Praise him for the times he's lifted you out of the pit of discouragement.

ALWAYS BE JOYFUL. KEEP ON PRAYING. NO MATTER WHAT HAPPENS, ALWAYS BE THANKFUL, FOR THIS IS GOD'S WILL FOR YOU WHO BELONG TO CHRIST JESUS.

1 THESSALONIANS 5:16-18

*F*ourteen years ago I didn't feel grateful when a speeding motorist hit my car, causing me subsequent pain for years afterward. Yet during that time, God gave me an empathy for those who live in pain—emotional, physical, or spiritual. Since then, he's brought many hurting people to my door.

A grateful heart generates inner peace, faith, and contentment, no matter the circumstances. Even in difficult times you can develop a fervent faith and a heart of genuine gratitude that pleases God.

Are You Truly Grateful?

As a young mom, I figured I had a lot to complain about. For ten years, my husband traveled continuously on business and left me alone to raise four children. It seemed as if every week the babies became ill, the older children fought, the washing machine conked out, or the car broke down! When things didn't go my way, I complained loud and long. I justified my behavior because juggling the roles of mom, housekeeper, nurse, chauffeur, referee, disciplinarian—and anything else that popped up—was far from easy!

One day during that bleak period, my Bible study teacher focused her lesson on two verses: "We know that God causes everything to work together for the good of those who love God and are called according to his purpose for them" (Rom. 8:28) and "No matter what happens, always be thankful" (1 Thess. 5:18). As I listened, I realized little genuine gratitude characterized my Christian life. Had my children dared to describe me in those days, they probably would have said, "Our mother is crabby all the time!"

Fortunately for my kids and my husband, I decided to forcibly remove the spotlight from myself and redirect my attention toward obeying and thanking God.

Yet even after several years of practicing gratitude, I was not grateful when a biopsy confirmed that my husband, Harlan, had cancer. We'd been happy and incredibly busy serving God. We couldn't imagine how cancer could ever work for our good and God's glory.

How could we guess that Harlan would experience twelve years of total remission—and that some of his finest ministry would occur during those years? No textbook ever contained the lessons we learned of faith, patience, endurance, and compassion. Eventually, we could echo Joseph's words in the Old Testament about his captivity in Egypt: "God turned into good what you meant for evil" (Gen. 50:20).

Then when a blood test disclosed my husband's skyrocketing cancer count, I again faced fear of the future. *Lord,* I prayed, *how will I handle it if you take my husband from me? Will I be able to praise you then?*

> *"Perfect" people are admired and put on pedestals, but it's real people we trust to struggle through the mud of our valleys with us.*
> PATRICIA DEVORSS

The years of practice I'd had in being grateful served me well one Tuesday morning when my husband's body could no longer fight the cancer. When the Lord took him home—with our four children surrounding me in a San Diego hospital room—I heard myself repeat the words of Job 1:21 with a choked voice: "The Lord gave me everything I had, and the Lord has taken it away. Praise the name of the Lord!"

My lifestyle of gratitude hasn't erased the learning curve of living alone and assuming responsibilities I've never faced before—hassling with finances, computing income tax, servicing my car, or checking the furnace. But my heart is at peace because I've decided to be grateful instead of bitter. And that's a choice anyone can make.   *Madalene Harris*

A STEP FURTHER

Developing an Attitude of Gratitude

1. *Deliberately choose to give thanks.*
   Memorizing 1 Thessalonians 5:18 can
   help: "No matter what happens, always
   be thankful, for this is God's will for you
   who belong to Christ Jesus."
2. *Focus on God, not your circumstances.* No
   matter the situation, we can find joy by
   transferring even a "hopeless" condition
   to God—and his goodness.
3. *Look on the bright side.* Don't miss chances
   to be grateful, such as when someone
   is kind to you or when an event turns
   out well. Resist looking for reasons to
   be critical, skeptical, or cynical.
4. *Wait and see.* Thank God in advance—
   before you see or know the conse-
   quences. God specializes in working
   things out for our good and his glory.

MH

Faith Focus

Do you tend to look at things negatively? Do you doubt God's wisdom? his concern for you? his ultimate control over the world? If your life is characterized by worry, anger, self-pity, or a judgmental, complaining spirit, how can you begin to generate the inner peace, faith, contentment, and positive attitude that please God and attract others?

Prayer Pointer

Ask God to help you focus less on yourself and your circumstances and more on grateful obedience to him. Thank him for opportunities to "practice gratitude" and pray that you will begin to develop fruits of a grateful heart, such as peace, contentment, and a positive spirit.

I WILL GIVE THEM SINGLENESS OF HEART AND PUT A NEW SPIRIT WITHIN THEM. I WILL TAKE AWAY THEIR HEARTS OF STONE AND GIVE THEM TENDER HEARTS INSTEAD, SO THEY WILL OBEY MY LAWS AND REGULATIONS. THEN THEY WILL TRULY BE MY PEOPLE, AND I WILL BE THEIR GOD.

EZEKIEL 11:19-20

*D*o you ever feel as if you're just going through the motions of being a Christian—that attending church, reading your Bible, serving others, and having a daily quiet time are only more "to-dos" for your schedule?

We all have times when we feel spiritually stagnant. But what really matters is what we choose to do about such times. Will we use them to discover more about God or to shelve our Bibles in a dusty spot?

When You Feel like a Fake

Several years ago, my spiritual life was stagnant. Although I wouldn't have admitted it then, I was spiritually bored. I knew there must be more to the Christian life than what I was experiencing—but I didn't know how to obtain it. Although I was a Christian and glad I could talk to God about the big things in life, the reality was, there weren't many big things happening. My life consisted of dishes, dust, and diapers.

After a lot of soul-searching, I realized that, despite the fact I'd become a Christian at twelve and had attended church all my life, much of what I had stuffed into my head had never dropped into my heart. I went through periods when I'd get excited about my faith; then my enthusiasm would wane. It wasn't until I began to meet God through prayer and reading his Word—instead of just "doing my quiet time" as a habit—that I began to grow as a Christian.

Instead of just memorizing Scripture "because I should," I began to memorize Scripture and pray over it, asking God to bring it to mind throughout the day so I could apply it to my life. Often I'd write out one of its applications and put it on the top of my prayer list. Then I'd think about ways to use it during the day in conversations with other people. God's Word began to transform my actions, thoughts, and words.

And the more I immersed myself in Scripture, the more I longed for time alone with God. I've learned to approach my time with God with the prayer of Psalm 119:18, which says, "Open my eyes to see the wonderful truths in your law." I began to ask the Lord to show me my "wonderful truth" for that day. Sometimes he gave me a particular verse to help me during the day or an insight into Scripture.

But I discovered that when I had this kind of time with God, his Word and the prayer needs of others were brought to mind throughout the day. Someone has put it well: Your time alone with God helps ensure a twenty-four-hour walk with him.

> *Our responsibility is to do faithfully what we believe God has called us to do. His responsibility is to fulfill those plans in response to our faithfulness, according to his perfect timing.*
>
> JUDY DOUGLASS

We have to remember that the Enemy doesn't want us to walk with God. When an extra hour opens up in our day—a perfect hour to be with the Lord—we have a choice as to how to spend it. Unless we have a deep need to know God better and cultivate our relationship with him, it's easy to spend free time doing housework or making phone calls. So I've found that I need to schedule time with God the same way I schedule other appointments. But I also need to make him my first priority. If I'm to love the Lord my God with all my heart, soul, mind, and strength, I can't make our meeting optional. In order to love him, it's essential to spend time with him! *Carole Mayhall*

A Step Further

Make Your Faith Real

1. *Make your faith your own.* God doesn't have spiritual grandchildren; you must claim Jesus as your *personal* Savior (see Rom. 3:23).
2. *Increase your heart knowledge.* Knowing God's Word by heart is critical if you want to mature in the faith.
3. *Really get to know God.* Anticipate time alone with him through Bible reading and prayer as you would a meeting with a friend.
4. *Pray for a healthy appetite.* Ask God for a hunger for his Word, a thirst for his righteousness.
5. *Live out your faith authentically.* A good work is anything you do in the name of the Lord (see Col. 3:17).   CM

Faith Focus

Is your faith authentic, or do you sometimes feel like a fake? If you're in a spiritual slump, which of the following steps could you take to liven up your spiritual life?

- Schedule a consistent time with God.
- Learn portions of the Bible by heart.
- Keep a record of how God is working in your life on a day-to-day basis to change you to be more like him. Why not use this list for encouragement on days when you feel discouraged?

Prayer Pointer

Let this be your prayer: "I pray that Christ will be more and more at home in my heart as I trust in him. May my roots go down deep into the soil of God's marvelous love. . . . Then I will be filled with the fullness of life and power that comes from you" (based on Eph. 3:17-19).

"For I know the plans I have for you," says the Lord. "They are plans for good and not for disaster, to give you a future and a hope. In those days when you pray, I will listen. If you look for me in earnest, you will find me when you seek me."

Jeremiah 29:11-13

*W*hat kind of prayers do you pray? Do you ask for protection as you drive to work? Do you recite a prayer before breakfast or dinner? Do you pray with your kids at bedtime or regularly with a friend as you walk?

Prayer is a crucial part of our spiritual growth. Maybe if we realized that God *does* listen when we pray (Jer. 29:11-13), we'd treat the power of prayer with even more awe and a grateful spirit.

If you want to mature as a Christ follower, maybe it's time you moved beyond "safe" prayers to "dangerous" prayers.

Praying Dangerously

Each day we pray all kinds of prayers—from the safe or self-serving to the risky and exciting. When was the last time you prayed a "dangerous" prayer—a prayer that put your faith on the line and opened you up to God in a way you've never done before?

God loves to hear dangerous prayers—the kind of prayers that help us grow as Christians. If you've been keeping God at a safe distance in your prayer life, try praying one of the following "dangerous" prayers—and see how God in his wisdom will answer it:

Search me. There's an old adage that says, "Don't ask the question if you're not ready to hear the answer." A "search me" prayer is dangerous because when you ask God to search your heart for anything that displeases him, he will. So don't pray a "search me" prayer unless you're ready for that kind of exposure!

Break me. Ecclesiastes 3:3 says, "[There is] a time to tear down and a time to rebuild." There's always something in my life that needs to be torn down—whether it's discouragement or pride or insensitivity. If you want to be set free to follow Christ fully, then it's time to pray a "break me" prayer.

Stretch me. If you're tired of going nowhere spiritually or relationally, if your marriage is difficult, or your children are going through tough times and you're not sure how to cope, ask God to stretch your marriage, your parenting, your spiritual understanding, even your courage to walk with him in a new way. Strength of character is won only by those who respond to life's challenges by asking God to stretch them.

Lead me. When you get settled into a house, a career, a growing family, or future plans, it's tempting to avoid dangerous "lead me" prayers that may "unsettle" your life. But that's where faith comes in. We need to believe God loves us and wants to lead our life down a better, more God-focused path than we could ever lead ourselves.

When you say, "God, here's my life. I'll follow your promptings; I'll listen for the tugs of your Spirit"—you'll be surprised what can happen.

> *If we really understood the power that's released when we pray, we'd be on our knees half the day.*
> TERRY MEEUWSEN

Use me. This prayer says, "God, I'm available if you'd like to do something great through me. I'm available if you'd like to touch another life through me." "Use me" prayers are powerful. They create adventures. You never know what the result of these prayers will be, but they're worth the risk of praying, because when you ask God to use you, he will. And it's wonderful to be used by God.

Praying these five dangerous prayers says you mean business with God. When you prayerfully and courageously move out of your comfort zone, your spiritual life will never be the same. "Search me. Break me. Stretch me. Lead me. Use me." Pray these prayers and watch what God does. *Bill Hybels*

A Step Further

Prayer Power

1. *Pray for your unsaved neighbors.* Pray that God will use you in some small way to touch them with his presence.
2. *Pray for your coworkers.* Pray for those who are discouraged, for those who have just given birth to or adopted a child, for those who long to be married or are newly divorced.
3. *Pray for your church's leaders.* Include not only the pastors, elders, etc., but all the men and women who serve as teachers.
4. *Pray for the nation.* Pray for moral character in our government's leaders. Pray for the strength of the American family. Pray that as a nation we will turn once again toward God.   RCT

Faith Focus

Are you satisfied with your prayer life, or do you want to grow even closer to God? If you're longing for more intimacy with God, which of these prayers could you risk praying today?

- Search me.
- Break me.
- Stretch me.
- Lead me.
- Use me.

Prayer Pointer

Thank God that he's faithfully and lovingly working out his plans for your life (Ps. 138:8). Ask him to give you the courage to pray a dangerous prayer, and then wait in eager anticipation for the results!

THOSE WHO LIVE IN THE SHELTER
OF THE MOST HIGH WILL FIND
REST IN THE SHADOW OF THE AL-
MIGHTY. THIS I DECLARE OF THE
LORD: HE ALONE IS MY REFUGE,
MY PLACE OF SAFETY; HE IS MY
GOD, AND I AM TRUSTING HIM.

PSALM 91:1-2

*C*leaning house. Running errands. Spending time with friends and family. Starting a new ministry. Teaching Sunday school. Attending church services. Singing in the choir. Working a full-time or part-time job. Shuttling kids to piano lessons or meals to elderly neighbors.

When you look at all we women do, no wonder we sometimes long for a rest! How wonderful that God knows us and gives us the promise of Psalm 91:1: "Those who live in the shelter of the Most High will find rest in the shadow of the Almighty." If you need a rest, take time out with God!

Need a Rest?

The headlights of my car were overpowered by the dense night as I crept along the mountain road. I peered through the rain-splattered windshield, unsure if the rain or my tears were making visibility so difficult.

Oh, God, why did this happen? I cried. I was returning from a visit with my parents and single younger sister who live several hours away. My sister had been severely brain-injured in a drunk driving accident eighteen months ago. Since then, I'd grabbed at every tiny sign of progress, full of irrational hope for her recovery. But on this visit, I was forced to face reality: My sister would never recover. For the rest of her life, she'd require constant care.

Grief consumed me as I twisted my way through the mountain pass. Shifting to a lower gear, I heard a loud thunk. Startled, I tried to shift into a different gear, but nothing happened. The car slowed to a standstill along the edge of the road.

Swallowing back fear, I locked the car and walked toward a gleam of light tucked back in the towering pine trees. It turned out to be the window of a small cottage. I approached the porch cautiously, hesitant to knock on an unfamiliar door late at night.

In response to my timid rap, the door swung open to reveal a middle-aged man. "Come in!" he welcomed. I hovered near the door, explained about my car, and asked to use his phone. When I dug out my calling card, he objected. "Your call's on me. I get lots of stranded people knocking on my door out here. It's my way of helping."

My phone call to my husband went unanswered, so I

asked the man if he knew of a motel nearby. "No motels," he said, "but I have an idea."

Before I knew it, I was handed over to the elderly owner of a nearby fishing lodge who had a room available. She, too, refused to take money.

The "room" actually was a cabin with one entire wall of glass overlooking a magnificent rushing river. A plump couch and chair faced a fireplace where a fire was laid, just waiting for me to strike a match.

Sitting there, warmed by the fire and relaxed by the sound of tumbling water, I opened my Bible to Psalm 139. By the third verse, my tears splashed onto the page. "You chart the path ahead of me and tell me where to stop and rest. Every moment you know where I am."

> *Every woman battles with the whirl of busyness and can benefit from holding her own restoration time with God.*
>
> PEGGY GRANT

As I contemplated the words, God spoke to my heart: *I'll give you the strength to endure your sister's tragedy, and I'll guide you through your sorrow—but tonight, stop and rest with me.*

Before I fell asleep, I called home to leave a message on the answering machine for my husband: "The car broke down on the mountain tonight. Please come and get me—but don't hurry. God and I are resting."

Mayo Mathers

A Step Further

A Rest Stop with God

1. *Set aside a four-hour (or more) time when you can get away from everything*—work, children, friends, family.
2. *A week ahead, prepare by reading your favorite portions of Scripture for a few minutes a day.* This helps prepare your heart for intimacy with God.
3. *Get away from your home, where distractions abound.* Go to a park, rent a hotel room. Use your creativity!
4. *Bring only your Bible, a pen, and notepad.* Resist the temptation to write "to-dos" on your paper. Instead, journal thoughts and prayers to God.
5. *Read several psalms to quiet your heart before God.*
6. *Spend time in prayer.* Praise God for who he is. Thank him for what he's done and is doing. Bring any requests before him.

RCT

Faith Focus

Are you feeling frazzled, worn-out with the "dailies" of living? What situations are making you weary these days? How might you make more rest for yourself—physically, emotionally, mentally, and spiritually? What steps do you need to take *today* to ensure that you get the rest you need?

Prayer Pointer

Praise God that he is not only your Savior but also your Shepherd who gives you everything you need, including rest (Ps. 23)! Ask him to help you be creative in getting the rest you need in all areas of your life.

Moses pleaded with the Lord, "O Lord, I'm just not a good speaker. I never have been, and I'm not now, even after you have spoken to me. I'm clumsy with words."

"Who makes mouths?" the Lord asked him. ". . . Is it not I, the Lord? Now go, and do as I have told you. I will help you speak well, and I will tell you what to say."

Exodus 4:10-12

$\mathcal{W}$hen someone talks about the importance of "sharing your faith," what's the first scene you envision?

- Standing on the street corner, passing out tracts.
- Going door to door (and maybe getting the door slammed in your face).
- Having to memorize a particular evangelism method before you can open your mouth.

There are many ways of talking with others about Christ. It can be as simple as sharing your testimony with a new friend or telling a child a Bible story. You don't need a soapbox or a tract to share your faith. You just need a willing mouth (Exod. 4:10-12)!

Good News!

I hate to admit it, but sometimes I'm afraid to open my mouth to tell others about Jesus. Oh, I love the Lord and want all my friends and family to know him—but when I try to witness, sometimes I feel as though a sock is stuffed down my throat.

If, like me, you feel guilty about not sharing Jesus' love with others but can't relate to traditional methods, there's another option I've found successful in leading several neighbors to Christ—lifestyle evangelism. I let my natural personality show neighbors the love of Christ as I walk with him moment by moment.

Scripture tells us that "no one can come to me unless the Father who sent me draws him" (John 6:44, NIV). This basic backdrop of truth to witnessing relieves me of the burden of perfectionism. It's God doing all the work—I'm just the vessel. As I align my life with him according to his Word, I can more easily hear God's voice and share how the Lord has intimately changed me.

Several years ago, I invited an unchurched friend, Marion, to our church. Unfortunately, the Sunday she and her husband attended, our church was going through an intense fund-raising drive. Marion wasn't interested in going back. But the Lord prompted me to invite her to go with me to a Bible study. At first I replied, "No way, Lord! She already gave church a try." But no matter how I tried, I couldn't shake the words, *Invite Marion!*

Finally I called her on the phone and said, "I feel God telling me to ask you to my Bible study. If you can't go or don't want to, I understand, but I can't get you out of my thoughts."

Surprisingly, she agreed and has been attending ever since (this is her fourth year). She accepted the Lord and now has more Bible knowledge than most lifelong Christians!

Lifestyle evangelism involves witnessing in word—and deed. You'll have a platform for sharing the gospel if you're also meeting others' needs. Why not have your children make a picture with a treat attached? Or maybe you can think of a book or tape that's appropriate to encourage a harried mom, a woman irritated with her husband, or a friend grieving a loss. Why not furnish welcome baskets with Bible verses attached for new neighbors? Unconditional love without expectation is a powerful testimony.

> *What a joy it would be to have someone say to you, down the road, "I learned about God through your love and belief in me!" So pass on godly legacies in your own home and community.*
>
> TWILA PARIS

Sharing the Good News can be an inconvenience, but God can't work through you if you're filled with self. To be an effective witness, you may have to drive out of your way to pick up a friend for church, but will losing a little sleep really kill you?

In the end, lifestyle evangelism's really about allowing the Lord to change and use you when you make your life available to him. There's no greater pleasure in life than to introduce someone else to God's grace.   *Suzy Ryan*

A STEP FURTHER

Simple Steps to Share Your Faith

1. *Ask the Lord whom he's drawing to himself—and how he can use you.* Pray he'll soften their hearts and give them saving faith.
2. *Obey God's promptings.* When God nudges you to share your faith, pray silently for his words. If all goes well, the Lord receives the glory. If disaster occurs, he takes responsibility. No pressure!
3. *Remember, people are watching.* Your neighbors will notice if you forgive a friend who treats you poorly or opt out of gossip sessions. When you choose to represent the Lord, you must hold yourself to a higher standard.
4. *Be committed to basic biblical truths, but don't get defensive.* If a friend wants to discuss abortion, for example, compassionately listen to her point of view, then share what Scripture says.   SR

Faith Focus

How often do you share your faith with others? Are you comfortable doing it? When you hear the word *witnessing,* what comes to your mind? What are some ways—small and big—you can think of to show others what God is like? How can you tell them about the Good News through your words and actions?

Prayer Pointer

Thank God for his incredible gift—the death and resurrection of his Son. Praise him for preparing a place for those who have accepted that sacrifice. Ask him to give you a knowledge of the truth, a willing mouth, and a love for the lost as you tell others the Good News.

ACKNOWLEDGMENTS

Today's Christian Woman magazine and Tyndale House Publishers would like to thank TCW staff members Barbara Calvert, Joy McAuley, and Linda Piepenbrink for their help in the editorial/permission process and the following people who graciously gave their permission to adapt the following material from *Today's Christian Woman* in this book.

Barker, Laura J. "Will You Pray for Me?" (July/August 1995).

Guest, Joan L. "What's Wrong with My Prayers?" (March/April 1986).

Halseide, Michele. "The Perfect Dad" (May/June 1991).

Harris, Madalene. "Being Grateful" (March/April 1993).

Heim, Pamela Hoover. "Can Spiritual Blahs Be a Blessing?" (July/August 1991).

Higgs, Liz Curtis. "Spread the Word!" (March/April 1996).

Hybels, Bill. "Five Dangerous Prayers" (July/August 1992); "Experiencing God's Emotions" (September/October 1995).

Liautaud, Marian V. "What's the Big Deal about Being a Christian?" (November/December 1995); "There's No Place like Home" (January/February 1997).

Mathers, Mayo. From *AfterWords*: "Before the Parade Passes By" (July/August 1995); "A Resting Place" (September/October 1995); "The Praise Connection" (March/April 1997); "My Father's the Best" (May/June 1997).

Mayhall, Carole. "When You Feel like a Fake" (November/December 1992); "Are You a Behind-the-Scenes Christian?" (May/June 1996); "Looking Back" (March/April 1997).

Menehan, Kelsey D. "Dealing with Doubt" (July/August 1996).

Mittelstaedt, Elizabeth. From *AfterWords:* "Living by God's Promises" (January/February 1995).

Newenhuyse, Elizabeth Cody. "When Good Things Happen to Bad People" (September/October 1996).

Patterson, Lauretta. "Everyday Idols" (September/October 1992); "I Don't Feel like a Very Good Christian" (July/August 1993).

Piepenbrink, Linda. "Why Ask Why?" (March/April 1990).

Ryan, Suzy. "Good News!" (September/October 1997).

Smith, Susan M. "How Does Your Garden Grow?" (July/August 1997).

Strobel, Lee. "Silent Nights" (November/December 1993).

Tada, Joni Eareckson. "The Major Problem with 'Minor' Sins" (May/June 1991).

Tucker, Ramona Cramer and Linda Piepenbrink. Interview with Anne Graham Lotz. "Rooted in the Word" (July/August 1996).

Van Reken, Ruth E. "The Truth about Spirituality" (November/December 1996).

Wright, Vinita Hampton. "Count on It!" (March/April 1996).